AF316656

CONSENT

THE FUNDAMENTAL CONCEPT

ASHISH SHEKHAR

Contents

Contents

Author

Ashish Shekhar is a multifaceted creative professional, excelling as a Professor, Content Writer, and Filmmaker. Armed with a Bachelor's degree in Mass Media and a Master's in Filmmaking, Shekhar's expertise spans the entertainment industry. He pursues further education in Advanced Filmmaking and Acting, showcasing his dedication to his craft. Shekhar's literary contributions include thought-provoking books like 'The Power of Portrayal - Movies & Culture', 'Ink and Echoes', and 'Knock Up Parable'. His research papers delve into contemporary societal dynamics, exploring topics like 'Songs dismissing Consent Culture' and 'Impact of Social Media on Youth'. Shekhar's storytelling prowess shines through diverse short films such as 'Heels', 'LoveShastra', and '702', earning him numerous awards. His poetry books reflect intricate emotions and reflections, resonating with readers across backgrounds. Alongside his creative pursuits, Shekhar is dedicated to nurturing aspiring storytellers and imparting knowledge and inspiration. What sets him apart is his belief in the unity of humanity, transcending barriers of caste, race, and colour through his work. Shekhar's commitment to inclusivity and celebration of diversity fosters global understanding through storytelling, making him a guiding light in literature and cinema.

Disclaimer

"In the comprehensive array of case studies and real-life examples presented in this book, meticulous care has been taken to source information solely from official statements and public domain laws and judgments. Each incident and legal decision discussed within these pages is rooted in verifiable data and authenticated sources, ensuring accuracy and reliability. However, it's imperative to recognize that laws and societal conditions are subject to evolution over time. As such, the interpretations of laws and judgments, as well as societal attitudes, may shift in response to changing circumstances and cultural dynamics. Therefore, to remain abreast of the most current legal precedents and societal norms, readers are encouraged to regularly consult official statements released by authoritative sources such as the press or media. By doing so, individuals can ensure that their understanding of legal principles and social dynamics remains up-to-date and informed."

Preface

Consent is the foundation of all respectful and meaningful human interactions. It is the unspoken understanding that facilitates our daily transactions, guaranteeing that the autonomy of each person is recognized and preserved. This book seeks to explore the nuanced definition of consent, the various forms it takes, and the degree to which it is critical to the formation of a civilized and compassionate society. Consent stretches across numerous domains. Whether it be the explicitly voiced consent associated with medical procedures or the unexpressed yet essential expectation of interactions with others, total comprehension, and implementation of the process of consent is necessary.

This notion is explored in this book by laying out these types of consent, how they operate, and why they are so imperative to social interaction at all levels. By providing an environment where issues of trust and respect are the norm, social order can be significantly improved by the recognition of consent. In the modern era, there is a greater demand for informed consent in several diverse spheres than at any other point in history. Items like online privacy, high-value concerns in the field of medicine, and even the simple reality that certain individuals require a higher degree of consent than others are all requirements for an in-depth understanding of this subject. This book reflects these realities by trying to show that informed consent, whether it be on legal, moral, or other issues, is never a bad idea. Consent is the process of always ensuring a voice for each individual and honouring that voice, and the decisions have to be respected as much as possible. It is the tool that great, civilised societies use to thrive. Consent prevents abuse, rectifies imbalances of power, and even creates communities. This book examines the subject of consent as it relates to various modes of human organization in the hopes of exploring how the practice of consent and its ensuing benefit of equality, both before the law and in general, can be further facilitated.

The significance of consent applies to all human relationships, from personal to professional. Consent takes a stand in families and friendships as well as at home at work and in any romantic relationship. The book explores the interpretation of consent in all these spheres and provides useful information. Examples and situations are taken from life experience and the media to show the transforming power of consent, which is mutually beneficial and gratifying. Popular culture helps us perceive the meaning of consent. Films, TV shows, music, and books widely use relations and human interaction as the main topics. The book explores the sphere of popular culture to show its influence and its realistic interpretation.

To sum up, this preface serves as a guide to the process of understanding the application of consent in human life. One of the purposes of the book is to demonstrate its true meaning and its importance. I believe that a world as it is seen from the pages of the book is closer to ideal. The emphasis on consent as a disposition in humans' minds and actions is the right way. Nothing can improve as soon as respect and consideration of individuals' interests and boundaries come first. This preface was written to walk the path of understanding and reasoning with readers through a process of learning about the meaning of consent. It will help us to think about the problem and our role in what we do, why, and how while acting.

Introduction

Consent is a fundamental concept that touches nearly every aspect of human interaction. It is the cornerstone of respectful relationships, the bedrock of legal frameworks, and a vital component of personal autonomy. Yet, despite its importance, the understanding and practice of consent remain complex and, at times, contentious. This book aims to unravel the multifaceted nature of consent, exploring its implications, challenges, and applications in various contexts.

> *"Consent is like borrowing a toothbrush – you definitely need to ask first. It's the difference between a hug and a surprise wrestling match. Think of it as a VIP pass to someone's comfort zone, not an all-access backstage ticket. Without it, you're just the annoying pop-up ad of human interactions!"*

In a world where power dynamics, cultural norms, and individual experiences shape our perceptions, consent is often misunderstood or misrepresented. This book seeks to clarify what consent truly means: a clear, enthusiastic, and informed agreement between parties. It is not merely a checkbox or a one-time transaction but an ongoing, dynamic process that requires communication, empathy, and mutual respect.

We begin with the in-depth definition and then examine the historical and legal evolution of consent, tracing its roots from ancient practices to modern-day statutes. This foundation helps us understand how societal changes influence our current interpretations and the legal protections in place. Next, we delve into the psychological and emotional dimensions of consent, exploring how personal boundaries, past experiences, and societal pressures impact individuals' ability to give or withhold consent.

One of the core objectives of this book is to highlight the importance of consent beyond the realm of sexual interactions. While consent in sexual relationships is crucial and often the focal point of discussions, we extend the dialogue to include medical consent, consent in digital spaces, and consent in everyday social interactions. By broadening the scope, we aim to foster a comprehensive understanding that empowers individuals to navigate their personal and professional lives with confidence and respect for others' autonomy.

Throughout the chapters, we feature real-life stories and case studies that illustrate both positive and negative examples of consent in action. These narratives provide practical insights and underscore the real-world consequences of consent violations. They also offer hope, showing how societies can evolve to prioritize and respect individual autonomy.

In this book, we also address the contentious issues surrounding consent, such as the impact of intoxication, the role of implicit versus explicit consent, and the challenges of consent in power-imbalanced relationships. By confronting these difficult topics, we aim to equip readers with the tools to engage in informed and compassionate discussions.

Ultimately, this book is a call to action. It encourages readers to reflect on their own understanding of consent, to educate themselves and others, and to advocate for practices and policies that uphold the dignity and autonomy of every individual. Whether you are a parent, educator, professional, or simply a concerned citizen, this book provides valuable insights and practical advice for fostering a culture of consent.

As you turn these pages, we invite you to join us on a journey toward a more respectful, equitable, and consent-conscious world.

ONE
CONSENT

because 'Yes' is sexy and 'No' is a full sentence

Hey, 'No' is the shortest complete sentence in the English language. Coincidence? I think not."

Let's unpack the first gem of wisdom: "Yes is sexy." Imagine this: you're at a concert, the music is thumping, the atmosphere is electric, and you ask your partner if they want to dance. They say, "Yes!" That enthusiastic consent? It's like a VIP pass to the dance floor of mutual respect and enjoyment. When someone says "Yes," it's not just a green light; it's a neon sign flashing, "I'm into this!" There's nothing sexier than knowing your partner is just as excited and willing as you are. It's like ordering pizza and finding out they threw in extra cheese for free - everybody wins!

Now, let's move to the powerhouse of brevity: "No is a full sentence." You don't need to be an English major to appreciate the beauty of this one. Picture yourself at a bakery, eyeing a delicious-looking cupcake. The baker says, "It's the last one." You ask, "Can I have it for free?" The baker simply says, "No." That's it. End of conversation. No need for excuses or justifications. It's clear, concise, and definitive. In the realm of consent, "No" doesn't need a sidekick. It stands strong on its own, like a superhero in a solo movie. It's empowering to know that your "No" is respected without needing to explain or apologize. It's like turning down a friend's offer to go skydiving because, well, no thanks - solid ground is just fine.

Let's sprinkle in some humour here. Remember, asking for consent isn't like filling out tax forms; it's about making sure everyone's on the same page and having a good time. Think of it as ordering from a menu with a friend. You wouldn't order them a ghost pepper pizza without checking if they're into spicy food first, right? Consent is your way of saying, "Hey, do you like this dish too?" and their response helps ensure you both enjoy the meal. Besides, nothing kills the mood faster than assuming someone wants anchovies on their pizza when they're clearly a pepperoni person.

So, the next time you're in a situation where consent matters (which, spoiler alert, is every situation involving another person), remember: "Yes" is not just permission; it's an enthusiastic, "I'm in!" And "No" isn't up for debate; it's a complete, unassailable declaration. Because at the end of the day, mutual consent is the ultimate recipe for a deliciously respectful and enjoyable experience. And who doesn't want that?

TWO
GET CONSENT

because 'I was just kidding' is for jokes, not boundaries

Ah, consent. The magical word that transforms you from an overbearing buffoon into a considerate and respectful human being. Imagine walking into a comedy club where the performer reads minds and only tells jokes you're absolutely okay with hearing. Wouldn't that be amazing? That, my friends, is the essence of consent - ensuring everyone involved is comfortable, on board, and ready to laugh (or cry, or have sex or anything else).

Picture this: you're at a party, and someone tries to pull off an impromptu magic trick by pulling a rabbit out of your hat, except you're not wearing a hat, and there's no rabbit, and you definitely didn't sign up to be part of a magic show. Awkward, right? This is precisely why consent is crucial. Just as a magician wouldn't force you into their act without a nod, we shouldn't assume participation without explicit agreement. "I was just kidding" works for the latest office prank where you swapped pens, not when you've stepped over someone's personal boundaries like an elephant in a tutu.

Speaking of jokes, let's dive into the classic "I was just kidding" defence. It's the equivalent of throwing a pie in someone's face and then claiming it's a new skincare treatment. Sure, it's funny in cartoons, but in real life, it's just messy and unwelcome. Jokes are meant to make people laugh, and not feel uncomfortable or disrespected. If your humour crosses into someone else's personal space without their go-ahead, it stops being a joke and starts being a problem. Remember, boundaries are not optional punchlines.

Let's keep the party metaphor going. Imagine hosting a dinner where you've prepared a gourmet spread, but instead of asking if anyone has allergies or dietary restrictions, you just serve peanut butter lasagna and hope for the best. Spoiler alert - someone's going to end up in the ER, and it won't be pretty. Consent is your pre-dinner checklist. It ensures that everyone has a good time and no one ends up metaphorically (or literally) choking.

So, next time you think about pulling the "I was just kidding" card, ask yourself - is this joke worth trampling over someone's comfort and trust? Instead, make consent your new punchline - it's always in good taste and guaranteed to get a genuine smile. After all, respect never goes out of style, and consent is the secret ingredient to any successful interaction, whether it's a joke, a conversation, or a magic trick gone right.

THREE
WINGMAN

**_Consent - the ultimate wingman - always
makes sure both parties are on board._**

Imagine consent as the James Bond of social interactions,
suave, sophisticated, and always in control. Just like 007
never embarks on a mission without a proper briefing,
neither should you dive into any intimate escapade without
the green light from both parties. Consent ensures that
everyone's on the same page, turning a potentially
awkward encounter into a mutual mission of delight. It's
the secret agent that stealthily diffuses any
misunderstandings and ensures smooth operations,
whether you're in the bedroom or just sharing a laugh over
a drink.

Consider consent as the unsung hero of every successful
rendezvous. It's like that friend who always checks if you're
okay to leave the party, but cooler and more integral to your
evening's success. Without consent, your romantic attempts

are like a plane trying to take off without clearance from air traffic control - a chaotic disaster waiting to happen. Instead, with consent at the helm, you're guaranteed a first-class ticket to a destination called mutual respect and enjoyment. And let's be honest, who doesn't want their interactions to fly smoothly without any turbulence?

Picture consent as a well-versed DJ, curating the perfect playlist for the night. You wouldn't want to drop a heavy metal track in the middle of a mellow jazz set, right? Just as a DJ reads the room and tunes into the vibe, consent keeps the groove going, ensuring that everyone is dancing to the same beat. It's about knowing when to drop the bass and when to slow things down, making sure the rhythm of the night is harmonious and enjoyable for all.

In the grand theatre of relationships, consent plays the role of a stellar stage manager. It ensures that the actors (that's you and your partner) know their lines, hit their marks, and feel comfortable in their roles. Without it, the performance could easily go off-script, leading to a show that's more cringe-worthy than captivating. But with consent, every act flows seamlessly, and the standing ovation at the end is guaranteed.

Consent isn't just a checkbox to tick off; it's the charismatic wingman who ensures that the evening's plans are smooth, exciting, and free of any awkward misunderstandings. It's the VIP pass to a night where everyone feels respected, heard, and ultimately, on board for the adventure. So, next time you're out and about, remember to bring your ultimate wingman along - after all, no great story ever started with someone being left out of the loop!

FOUR
SEEK

When in doubt, just ask. Communication is hotter than assumption.

"Assumptions are the termites of relationships." - Henry Winkler

Imagine this: you're in the kitchen, and your roommate has left a mysterious, unlabeled container in the fridge. It could be last night's lasagna, a science experiment gone awry, or, heaven forbid, the remnants of a failed attempt at kombucha. You stare at it, your mind swirling with possibilities. Do you dare to taste it, risking your taste buds and possibly your life? Or do you simply ask, "Hey, what's in the container?" The latter, my friends, is a prime example of why "When in doubt, just ask" is a golden rule of thumb. Communication saves you from playing culinary Russian roulette.

Now, let's dissect the notion that "communication is hotter than assumption." Think about the last time you assumed your partner knew exactly what you wanted for your birthday. You dropped subtle hints, posted Pinterest boards, and even left your Amazon wish list open on the shared laptop. Yet, come birthday morning, you find yourself holding a pair of socks with cats on them. Sure, cats are cute, but you were hoping for something a bit more... sparkly. Here's where the humour kicks in - assumptions are like those socks. They might cover the basics, but they rarely hit the mark. A direct conversation, however, is like gifting your partner a GPS with a direct route to your heart's desires. It's not just hotter, it's blazing with clarity and precision.

Picture this: you're on a date, and your date mentions they "love adventure." In your mind, you're already planning a surprise bungee jumping trip. Fast forward to date day, and their face goes from excited to horrified as they exclaim, "I meant watching adventure movies!" Ah, the sweet sting of assumptions! You see, asking clarifying questions not only prevents catastrophic misunderstandings but also ensures that your plans don't end up as fodder for a future awkward story.

Finally, let's not forget the workplace, where assumptions are the landmines of professional life. Bob from accounting sends an email asking for the "TPS report." Assuming it's due next week, you blissfully sip your coffee, only to discover at 4:59 PM that it was due, oh, right now. A simple "When do you need this by?" could have saved you from the frantic scramble and Bob's infamous death stare. In essence, communication is not just hotter, it's a lifesaver.

In the grand tapestry of human interaction, assumptions are the tangled knots, while communication is the skillful weaver's hand that smooths everything out. So next time you're faced with the unknown, embrace the heat of a good conversation. Ask the question, clear the doubt, and revel in the smooth, seamless fabric of understanding. And remember, even socks with cats can't save you from the perils of assumption.

FIVE
RESPECT

Respect boundaries - they're like invisible electric fences for bad decisions.

"Respect boundaries - they're like invisible electric fences for bad decisions."

Imagine you're a mischievous puppy, all bright-eyed and bushy-tailed, bounding through the yard without a care in the world. Everything seems like a chew toy and every corner is a new adventure. But there's this mysterious invisible electric fence in place, buzzing silently, a guardian angel disguised as a shockwave. It doesn't take long before you realize that crossing that line means a jolt - a not-so-subtle reminder that some adventures are best left unexplored. Boundaries in life work the same way. They're the gentle zaps that save us from the doghouse of regret, reminding us that not all shiny objects are meant to be chased.

Consider boundaries as the unsung heroes in the epic saga of human relationships. They might not wear capes, but they do a stellar job of keeping the drama llama at bay. Without boundaries, our lives would be an endless rerun of a sitcom where everyone's personal space and sanity are perpetually violated. Picture it: your nosy neighbour borrowing sugar at 3 AM, your boss expecting you to answer emails on Sunday morning, or your friend treating your closet like a free-for-all fashion boutique. It's chaos! Boundaries are the plot devices that keep these sitcom scenarios from spiralling into a never-ending comedy of errors.

Think of boundaries like a GPS for emotional navigation. Without them, you're like a driver ignoring the "bridge out" sign and plummeting into the ravine of awkward confrontations and resentment. "Turn back now!" it silently screams, but alas, without boundaries, we're all too often left fishing for forgiveness from the bottom of that proverbial ravine. By setting and respecting boundaries, we're essentially saying, "Hey, I'd rather not dive headfirst into that awkward abyss, thank you very much."

In the grand buffet of life, boundaries are like the sneeze guard. Without them, who knows what kind of germs (read: unwanted drama and emotional baggage) could land in your metaphorical potato salad? Sure, some people might think, "Who needs sneeze guards?" But one encounter with an unexpected sneeze topping on your favourite dish, and you're a believer. Similarly, once you've experienced the tranquillity that boundaries bring, you'll guard them like a dragon protects its treasure.

So, next time someone tries to cross your boundary, imagine yourself as a fortress with an electric moat. It's not about keeping people out; it's about keeping the harmony in. Boundaries aren't just barriers; they're the peacekeepers, the diplomats of our personal space. And remember, a well-placed boundary today saves a lot of apologies tomorrow. Embrace your inner puppy, learn to respect that electric fence, and keep your tail wagging happily on the safe side of sanity.

SIX
DON'T GUESS

Because guessing is for game shows, not relationships.

Guessing games are fun unless it's about what's for dinner or whether you locked the front door. But when it comes to relationships, guessing should be left to Wheel of Fortune, not the intimate dynamics of consent. Navigating the world of human connection without clear communication is like trying to put together IKEA furniture without instructions - confusing, frustrating, and likely to leave you with extra parts and a puzzled expression.

Imagine if every romantic advance came with a flashy game show soundtrack. "And now, for the grand prize, will they say 'yes' to dinner and a movie? Let's spin the wheel!" Cue the dramatic music and suspenseful pause. It sounds absurd, right? That's because consent isn't something you win by chance; it's a clear, mutual agreement that involves both parties being fully informed and enthusiastic. No one should have to cross their fingers and hope they guessed right.

Think of consent as the ultimate cheat code for relationships. It's like having a GPS for human interaction: "In 500 feet, turn left towards a comfortable conversation about boundaries." Without it, you're bound to get lost in a labyrinth of miscommunications and misunderstandings. Remember that one time you tried to mind-read your partner's mood and ended up on the couch watching reruns alone? Yeah, let's not repeat that.

It's important to remember that clarity is sexy. There's nothing more attractive than knowing exactly where you stand with someone. "Can I kiss you?" is not only a smooth line but also a surefire way to avoid the awkwardness of mixed signals. Plus, it shows you care about the other person's feelings - an underrated yet highly effective move in the romance playbook.

So, the next time you're in a situation that calls for consent, don't leave it up to chance. Ask the questions, have the conversations, and enjoy the peace of mind that comes with knowing everyone is on the same page. After all, guessing is best left for game shows, not the crucial aspects of our relationships.

SEVEN

INVISIBLE CONCEPT

The Invisible Concept of Consent with Visible Impact

Consent is a bit like oxygen - invisible and often taken for granted, but its absence is immediately and dramatically felt. Let's dive into this concept with a touch of a hypothetical scenario that highlights its importance.

Imagine a bustling office environment. Our protagonist, Alex, is an enthusiastic worker who loves surprising colleagues with random acts of kindness. One day, Alex decides to boost team morale by giving everyone surprise back massages. Sounds delightful, right?

Not quite.

Alex begins with Jamie, who is deeply engrossed in a project. Without a word, Alex starts massaging Jamie's shoulders. Jamie jumps, spilling coffee all over their desk.

"What are you doing?" Jamie exclaims, half-laughing, half-aghast.

"Just trying to help you relax!" Alex beams.

"Well, a little warning - or, you know, asking - would've been nice!" Jamie responds, now frantically wiping up the coffee.

Alex moves on, undeterred, to Taylor, who is on the phone with a client. As Alex's hands land on Taylor's shoulders, Taylor lets out a startled yelp, causing the client to ask if everything is alright. After a brief, awkward explanation, Taylor hangs up and turns to Alex with a forced smile.

"Alex, I appreciate the thought, but maybe save the surprise massages for off-hours, okay?"

Finally, Alex approaches Sam, who is notorious for having a significant personal space bubble. Before Alex can even get close, Sam backs away with wide eyes.

"Nope, nope, nope! Personal space, Alex!"

In this scenario, the concept of consent is invisible - there's no neon sign flashing "ASK FIRST"- but its impact is very much visible. Alex's well-meaning but misguided attempts to help visibly disrupt the office, causing spills, awkward explanations, and discomfort.

The humour here lies in the absurdity of assuming everyone would be delighted by unexpected massages. It's clear that without the invisible but crucial step of asking for consent, Alex's actions result in visible chaos and discomfort.

Now, imagine if Alex had approached this differently:

Alex walks up to Jamie. "Hey Jamie, I noticed you're really focused. Would you like a quick shoulder massage, or would that be too distracting?"

Jamie smiles, "Thanks, Alex, but I'm good. Appreciate the offer, though!"

Moving on to Taylor, Alex waits for the call to end and asks, "Taylor, would you like a shoulder massage?"

Taylor replies, "That's nice of you, Alex, but maybe another time."

Finally, Alex stops by Sam's desk. "Sam, would you be interested in a shoulder massage to help with the stress?"

Sam chuckles, "No thanks, Alex, but I appreciate you asking!"

In this revised version, Alex's respectful approach to consent not only prevents disruption but also strengthens workplace relationships. The invisible concept of consent becomes a visible practice of respect and consideration, demonstrating that while consent itself might be unseen, its positive impact is unmistakable.

So, remember, whether it's a shoulder massage, sharing a secret, or something more significant, always make the invisible visible: ask for consent. Because as Alex learned, what's unseen can have very real and very visible effects.

EIGHT

BOB'S AWAKENING

The Invisible Concept of Consent - A Woman's Perspective

Imagine a bustling office environment where our protagonist, Emily, navigates her day with a blend of professionalism and a dash of humour. Emily, like many women, has mastered the art of dodging unwanted advances and mansplaining with the finesse of a matador.

Enter Bob. Bob is well-meaning but has the subtlety of a sledgehammer. He's convinced that his every interaction is a gift to womankind, never pausing to consider that maybe, just maybe, consent is a thing.

Scene One: The Coffee Machine Conundrum

Emily is at the coffee machine, savouring her five minutes of peace. Bob saunters over, grinning like he's just discovered fire.

"Hey, Emily! Let me get that for you," he says, reaching for the coffee pot.

Emily smiles politely. "Thanks, Bob, but I got it."

But Bob's already pouring, and in his enthusiasm, coffee spills everywhere. Emily steps back, internally sighing.

"Bob, you know, I appreciate the help, but sometimes a girl just wants to pour her own coffee without it turning into a slapstick routine."

Scene Two: The Compliment Catastrophe

Later, in a meeting, Emily presents a well-researched proposal. As she finishes, Bob leans in, completely missing the point.

"Emily, great job! And by the way, that dress really brings out your eyes."

Emily's smile tightens. "Thanks, Bob. And your tie really brings out the... colour of your shirt."

It's not that Bob's comment was inherently awful, but it's a classic example of how men often overlook the need for professional respect over unsolicited personal commentary. Emily thinks, "Ah, the invisible concept of consent strikes again. Compliment my work, not my wardrobe, Bob."

Scene Three: The Unsolicited Shoulder Massage

Then comes the pièce de résistance. Emily's at her desk, deep in thought, when she feels two hands on her shoulders. Bob strikes again with his unsolicited shoulder massage.

"Relax, Emily. You're working too hard," he says, oblivious to the way she stiffens.

"Bob, unless you've magically turned into my spa therapist, hands off. Seriously, did you miss the memo on personal space?"

Bob chuckles, clueless. "Just trying to help."

Emily smiles sweetly, thinking, "Help? If I needed help, I'd ask. Ever heard of the invisible concept of consent, Bob? It's like common sense, but rarer."

Scene Four: The Mansplaining Moment

Emily is explaining her project to the team when Bob interrupts, explaining her own idea back to her.

"Actually, Emily, what you're trying to say is…"

Emily raises an eyebrow. "Wow, Bob, I never thought of my own idea that way. Thanks for mansplaining it to me."

The room chuckles, and Bob finally gets it. Sort of.

Emily's Day is a microcosm of a larger issue: the invisible concept of consent, especially in the context of women's experiences with men who don't quite get it. It's not just about the grand gestures, but the small, everyday interactions where men often fail to see the importance of asking, of respecting boundaries, of recognizing that consent isn't just for the big things - it's for everything.

In the grand theatre of life, consent might be an invisible actor, but its absence? That's a showstopper. So, guys, take a cue from Emily's day - don't just assume - ask. Because whether it's coffee, compliments, or contact, consent makes everything run smoother. And who knows, you might just avoid being the next Bob.

NINE

ONLY 'YES' MATTERS

"In the grand dance of human interaction, there's one word that serves as both the melody and the rhythm: consent. It's the cornerstone of respect, the guardian of boundaries, and the ultimate arbitrator of 'yes' in the tangled ballad of relationships. But let's not confine this crucial concept solely to the confines of bureaucracy or contracts; oh no, it's a star performer in the most intimate of arenas - the bedroom!"

Picture this: two consenting adults, ready to embark on a journey through the labyrinth of pleasure. But wait! Before you break out the champagne or start the steamy soundtrack, there's a crucial step - the consent waltz. It's not just a mere formality; it's the overture to a symphony of mutual desire and satisfaction. Think of it as the prelude to a passionate sonnet, with each 'yes' harmonizing perfectly with the other.

Now, let's debunk a myth or two while we're at it. Consent isn't a one-time offer or a rubber stamp for unlimited access; it's more like a VIP pass with strict terms and conditions. And believe me, those terms are non-negotiable. No means no, but let's not forget the glorious variations of 'yes' - the enthusiastic 'yes', the hesitant 'yes', and the downright excited 'YES!' Each one deserves a round of applause, a standing ovation even, because in this theater of pleasure, every 'yes' is a star performer.

Ah, but here's where it gets even more intriguing – consent isn't just about the absence of a 'no'. It's about active participation, about checking in with your partner as if you're both navigating a particularly tricky IKEA assembly manual together. 'Are you comfortable?' 'Is this what you want?' These aren't just lines from a romance novel; they're the sweet, sweet melody of consent serenading us to a crescendo of mutual delight.

So, my friends, let's raise our glasses to consent - the unsung hero of romance, the champion of respect, and the only 'yes' that truly matters, especially when the lights are low and the mood is just right. Let's make consent the sexiest word in the dictionary, shall we? After all, a little humor, wit, and a whole lot of yes-ness make for a darn good time in the bedroom - or anywhere else, for that matter!

Remember, 'yes' means 'yes,' not 'maybe' or 'I guess.'

When someone says "yes," it's like popping a champagne cork of affirmation. It's a resounding declaration of commitment, a verbal high-five, a green light in the traffic of life. "Yes" is the superhero cape of words, swooping in to rescue plans from the clutches of uncertainty.

But alas, sometimes "yes" gets a little lost in translation. It's like it puts on a disguise and sneaks into conversations as a timid "maybe" or a wishy-washy "I guess." It's the ninja of consent, slipping through the shadows of hesitation.

So, when we say "yes means yes," it's not just a gentle reminder; it's a battle cry for clarity! It's a declaration that when you hear that magical word, there's no need to consult a crystal ball or decode hidden messages. It's a call to arms against the army of ambiguity, armed with sarcasm and shields of scepticism.

And let's face it, life is too short for guessing games. We've got better things to do - like pondering the mysteries of the universe or perfecting our pancake-flipping technique. So, let's embrace the power of "yes" with open arms and a firm handshake. After all, in a world of maybes and I guesses, a solid "yes" is a diamond in the rough, a beacon of certainty in a sea of uncertainty. So, let's raise our glasses (filled with whatever beverage suits your fancy) and toast to the unequivocal power of "yes!"

TEN

SHOULDN'T BE HARD

the only thing that should be hard during sex is the conversation.

Ah, what a cheeky yet crucial statement! Let's dissect this saucy nugget, shall we? First off, the quote sets the tone perfectly - consent is key, and the only thing that should be stiff (pun intended) during the act is the actual discussion about it.

Now, let's talk about consent. It's not the sexiest topic, but it's undoubtedly the most important. Consent is like the salt in a dish - it might not be the star ingredient, but without it, the whole thing falls flat. It's not just about asking "yes or no?" in a robotic manner; it's about enthusiastic, ongoing, and clear communication. Picture this: you're about to engage in some amorous activities, and instead of the usual pre-game banter, you whip out a consent contract with fine print and a signature line. Not exactly the mood setter, right?

So, what's the alternative? Well, imagine this instead - you and your partner are getting cozy, things are heating up, and you throw in a playful, "Is this okay?" or "You like that?" It's like adding a sprinkle of flirtation to the mix. Plus, it opens up a dialogue where both parties feel comfortable expressing their desires, and boundaries, and maybe even throwing in a few suggestions for good measure.

Now, onto the "hard" part. No, not *that* hard. We're talking about the conversation. Let's face it, talking about consent can sometimes feel as awkward as trying to assemble IKEA furniture without the instructions. But hey, it doesn't have to be that way. Think of it as a chance to showcase your communication skills - you know, the ones you listed on your dating profile under "special talents."

And here's where the humour kicks in. Imagine fumbling through the consent talk like a nervous teenager trying to parallel park for the first time. It's like a comedy of errors, with awkward pauses, nervous laughter, and maybe even a few accidental double entendres thrown in for good measure. But hey, laughter is the best aphrodisiac, right?

So, let's recap - consent is non-negotiable, but that doesn't mean the conversation has to be as stiff as a board. Keep it light, keep it playful, and most importantly, keep it consensual. After all, there's nothing sexier than mutual respect and open communication. Now, go forth and conquer - with consent, of course!

ELEVEN
MANTRA

If it's not a 'heck yes,' it's a definite 'heck no'- that's the consent mantra.

The timeless wisdom of the 'heck yes' consent mantra! It's like the decisive battle cry of enthusiastic agreement, isn't it? Picture this - you're standing at the crossroads of decision-making, faced with choices ranging from 'meh' to 'absolutely heck yes!' That's where this mantra swoops in, cape flapping in the breeze of your uncertainty, ready to rescue you from the land of lukewarm commitments.

Imagine you're at a taco stand, contemplating whether to order that extra side of guac. Should you? Well, if the mere thought of that creamy, avocado goodness doesn't elicit a resounding 'HECK YES!' from the depths of your soul, then perhaps it's time to save your pesos for another culinary adventure. Because let's face it, life's too short for mediocre guacamole.

Now, let's apply this mantra to matters of the heart, shall we? Picture a first-date scenario. You're sipping your latte, nervously twirling your straw, and your date suggests a spontaneous salsa dancing class. Your reaction? If your inner monologue doesn't scream 'HECK YES!' louder than the beat of a reggaeton track, then maybe it's best to politely decline and save yourself from the potential embarrassment of tripping over your own two feet. Hey, nobody wants to perform the cha-cha of awkwardness on a first-date dance floor!

But wait, there's more! This mantra isn't just reserved for taco toppings and romantic rendezvous. Oh no, it extends to all facets of life. Picture yourself contemplating a career change. Should you take that leap into the unknown? Well, if the mere thought of pursuing your passion doesn't ignite a fiery 'HECK YES!' within you, then maybe it's time to reassess your options. After all, life's too short to spend your days dreaming of what could have been while you're stuck in cubicle purgatory.

So, the next time you find yourself at the proverbial fork in the road, remember this mantra: if it's not a 'heck yes,' it's a definite 'heck no.' Embrace the enthusiasm, relish in the certainty, and let the power of decisive consent guide you towards a life filled with guacamole, salsa dancing, and pursuing your passions with unbridled gusto. Because why settle for anything less than a resounding 'HECK YES!' in a world brimming with endless possibilities?"

TWELVE

A SHOUT

Consent is not a whisper, it's a shout - make sure you're listening.

Picture this - you're at a noisy party, music blasting, people chatting, and suddenly, in the midst of all the chaos, someone whispers, "Hey, can I borrow your phone?" Chances are, you might miss it entirely! Consent, much like that request for a phone, isn't something you should strain to hear. It's not a subtle hint or a quiet murmur; it's a loud, clear declaration. Imagine if every time someone wanted your attention, they whispered from across the room - it'd be chaos! Similarly, consent should be unmistakable, unmistakably loud. So, if you find yourself straining to hear it, you're doing it wrong! Maybe invest in some metaphorical hearing aids, or better yet, just pay attention!

Now, let's dissect this idea a bit further. Picture yourself in a situation where you're deciding what movie to watch with a friend. They suggest a horror flick, and you reply with a resounding "Yes!" Easy, right? But what if they suggest something you're not so keen on? Maybe a rom-com that makes your eyes roll faster than a tumbleweed in a desert storm. In that case, you might muster up a weak, hesitant "Uh, sure, I guess." But hold on a second! Is that really consent? Or is it just the path of least resistance? Consent, my friend, is not about reluctantly going along with something; it's about enthusiastically saying, "Hell yeah!" or confidently asserting, "Nope, not my cup of tea!" So, next time you're faced with a movie dilemma, remember - be as decisive as a kid in a candy store, and if you're not feeling it, shout it from the rooftops -metaphorically, of course.

And let's not forget the humorous side of things. Picture this - a scenario straight out of a sitcom - two friends, one asking the other for a favour. "Hey, can I borrow your pet goldfish for my synchronized swimming class?" The request hangs in the air, waiting for a response. But instead of a clear answer, there's silence, crickets chirping in the background. The asker squints, trying to decipher the mumbled response, but it's too late - the moment has passed, and the goldfish remains safe in its bowl. Moral of the story? If you're gonna ask for something, make sure you do it loud and clear, like a carnival barker announcing the greatest show on earth! And if you're on the receiving end, channel your inner rock star and belt out your response because in the grand symphony of consent, silence is not music to anyone's ears!

THIRTEEN

SHOULDN'T SKIP

If you wouldn't put pineapple on someone's pizza without asking, you definitely shouldn't skip asking for consent.

The timeless debate over the sanctity of pizza toppings and the importance of consent! As the great philosopher of modern times, Unknown, once wisely stated, 'If you wouldn't put pineapple on someone's pizza without asking, you definitely shouldn't skip asking for consent.' Let's embark on a journey to unravel the profound wisdom hidden within these seemingly unrelated concepts.

Firstly, consider the contentious issue of pineapple on pizza. Some adore the sweet and tangy flavour combination, while others cringe at the mere thought. It's akin to a culinary battleground, where factions clash over what constitutes acceptable toppings. Yet, in the midst of this cheesy chaos, one principle reigns supreme - respect for personal preference. Just as you wouldn't stealthily sneak pineapple onto a staunch anti-pineapple pizza enthusiast's pie (unless you're feeling particularly mischievous), you must approach matters of consent with equal care.

Now, onto the crux of the matter - consent. It's the cornerstone of any healthy relationship or interaction, whether in the realm of pizza toppings or matters far more consequential. Consent isn't merely a checkbox to tick off; it's a continuous dialogue, a mutual understanding, a dance of respect and communication. Just as you wouldn't slap a slab of pineapple onto a pizza without ensuring everyone's on board (unless you enjoy a side of chaos with your mozzarella), you shouldn't proceed with any action, be it physical or otherwise, without explicit consent.

But why the emphasis on asking for consent? Well, imagine the horror of sinking your teeth into a slice of pizza, only to be assaulted by an unexpected burst of fruity sweetness. Similarly, engaging in any activity without consent can lead to equally unpleasant surprises, albeit of a more serious nature. Consent ensures that everyone involved is not only willing but enthusiastically so, much like a pizza lover eagerly anticipating their favourite toppings.

Now, for a sprinkle of humour amidst this philosophical pondering. Picture this - you're at a pizza party, armed with a slice loaded with toppings galore. You confidently take a bite, only to discover that your friend, in a daring display of culinary rebellion, has surreptitiously adorned your slice with pineapple. The horror! The betrayal! Thus, the importance of consent becomes all too clear, whether in matters of pizza toppings or more profound human interactions.

Let us heed the sage advice encapsulated in the enigmatic words of Unknown - if you wouldn't impose pineapple on someone's pizza without asking, you certainly shouldn't skip asking for consent in any aspect of life. After all, in the grand buffet of existence, respect, communication, and consent are the essential ingredients for a truly satisfying feast.

FOURTEEN

CONSENT IN MARRIAGE

In marriage, 'I do' means 'I consent' - and that applies to everything from chores to Netflix choices.

Marriage - the ultimate partnership where 'I do' signifies not just a declaration of love but a commitment to consent to a lifetime of shared experiences. From the mundane to the magnificent, every aspect of married life hinges on those two little words. 'I do' - the magical incantation that binds two souls together in a dance of dishes and a tango of TV shows. But let's unpack this, shall we?

When you say 'I do,' you're essentially signing up for a lifetime subscription to compromise. Take chores, for instance. Gone are the days of solo dishwashing escapades or laundry adventures. Now, it's a collaborative effort, a choreographic masterpiece where one partner might excel at scrubbing toilets while the other conquers the art of folding fitted sheets. And if there's one thing marriage teaches you, it's that sometimes the chore wheel spins in mysterious ways, leaving you pondering the philosophical question - who forgot to take out the trash this time?

And, then there are the Netflix choices. Ah, the battleground of modern matrimony. 'I do' means 'I consent' to hours of negotiation over what to watch on TV. It's a delicate dance of diplomacy, where compromise reigns supreme. One night, you're binging a gripping crime drama while the next, you find yourself knee-deep in a rom-com marathon. But fear not, for in the sacred covenant of marriage, there's always room for a 'one for you, one for me' approach. Besides, isn't half the fun in pretending to be a film critic and dissecting the plot holes together?

But let's not forget the beauty of it all. In the grand tapestry of marriage, every 'I do' is a brushstroke, painting a picture of love, laughter, and the occasional load of laundry forgotten in the machine. It's about embracing the chaos, finding joy in the shared moments, and realizing that even in the most mundane tasks, there's magic to be found.

So, the next time you find yourself elbow-deep in dish suds or engaged in a heated debate over whether to watch a documentary or a comedy special, remember this - 'I do' isn't just a phrase - it's a promise. A promise to navigate the twists and turns of life together, armed with love, laughter, and maybe a little bit of Netflix-induced negotiation.

FIFTEEN

LACK OF CONSENT

In marriage, 'I'm too tired' is a legitimate reason for lack of consent...especially when it comes to doing the dishes.

In the grand theatre of marriage, where love and compromise pirouette in a perpetual dance, there are moments when exhaustion plays the role of the grand saboteur. As the curtains draw upon a long day's performance, and the actors of domesticity take their final bow, one might find themselves uttering those immortal words, 'I'm too tired.' Ah, yes, a phrase both revered and dreaded, for in its simplicity lies the power to halt even the most mundane of household chores. Yet, let us dissect this phrase, this tiny morsel of exhaustion wrapped in a blanket of legitimacy.

Picture this - a kitchen sink overflowing with the remnants of culinary conquests, each dish a testament to the gastronomic delights once enjoyed. And there, amidst the chaos, stands a weary soul, armed with nothing but a sponge and a weary sigh. 'I'm too tired,' they declare, their voice a weary lamentation to the burdens of the day. And truly, who can blame them? For in the battle of wills between a tired soul and a mountain of dishes, fatigue reigns supreme.

But fear not, dear reader, for within this seemingly mundane excuse lies a kernel of comedic gold. Imagine the absurdity of it all, the sheer audacity of exhaustion to render one incapable of wielding a scrub brush! Oh, the trials and tribulations of married life, where even the most trivial of tasks become epic battles of wills. And so, let us raise a toast to the tired souls of the world, those brave warriors who dare to utter those immortal words in the face of domestic duty.

Let it be known that in the realm of marriage, 'I'm too tired' is not merely an excuse, but a battle cry, a rallying call for the weary masses. And when it comes to doing the dishes, well, sometimes fatigue truly is the greatest of adversaries. So next time you find yourself faced with a sink full of plates and a heart full of exhaustion, remember this - you are not alone in your struggle. For in the grand tapestry of marriage, even the simplest of chores can become legendary tales of triumph and defeat. And in the end, isn't that what makes the journey all the more amusing?

I am too tired to be awake

In marriage, sometimes the most intimate conversations happen not in the bedroom, but in the moments where exhaustion reigns supreme. 'I am too tired,' a phrase whispered in the twilight of a long day, holds within it a multitude of meanings. Yes, it could signify the fatigue that weighs heavy on eyelids and limbs, but it also carries the unspoken agreement of mutual respect and understanding between partners. It's the unspoken code for 'let's hit the hay and tackle this tomorrow.' And let's be honest, if there's any 'tackling' happening, it's more likely to involve pillows than passion.

When 'I am too tired' extends to the realm of physical intimacy, it becomes a humorous nod to the realities of long-term commitment. Gone are the days of youthful exuberance where staying up all night was a badge of honour. Now, it's more about Netflix marathons and falling asleep halfway through. Besides, who needs the drama of a steamy romance novel when you can have the comfort of knowing your partner will bring you a glass of water and tuck you in?

Let's not forget the comedic potential of 'I am too tired' in the context of spousal negotiations. It's the ultimate trump card in the game of household chores. Want to avoid doing the dishes? 'Sorry, honey, I'm just too tired tonight.' Laundry piling up? 'I'd love to help, but you know, tiredness and all.' It's the marital equivalent of playing the exhaustion card in Monopoly - and just as effective.

So, while 'I am too tired' may seem like a simple statement, in the grand opera of marriage, it's a versatile aria, sung in the key of understanding, with a dash of humour and a sprinkle of shared experience. After all, in the symphony of life, sometimes the sweetest melody is the sound of two partners snoring in perfect harmony.

SIXTEEN
INTIMACY

Remember, 'I do' doesn't mean 'I always will' - check-in for the encore!

The symphony of matrimony! Picture this: a grand orchestral performance, the vows exchanged like a crescendo, and the grand finale? 'I do.' But hold your applause, folks, because as any maestro knows, the encore is where the magic truly happens!

Let's unpack this melodious metaphor, shall we? 'Remember, 'I do' doesn't mean 'I always will'- check-in for the encore!' Now, think of 'I do' as the overture, the prelude to a lifelong concert. It's that initial commitment, the moment when you say, 'Yes, I'm in for the long haul.' But - and here's where it gets interesting - life, like music, is full of surprises. Tempos change, melodies evolve, and sometimes, you find yourself in need of a remix.

Enter the encore, the spicy salsa to your marriage mambo! This is where you check back in, revitalize that rhythm, and perhaps even add a few new dance moves to the repertoire. See, 'I always will' isn't just a one-time declaration; it's an ongoing symphony of love, laughter, and, let's not forget, lust!

Now, about that encore - let's talk about the 'sex' part, shall we? Because, let's be honest, it's the electric guitar solo in this rock opera of marriage. Sure, it's not always centre stage, but when it is, oh boy, does it steal the show! So, don't just settle for the opening act. Check in for that encore performance, and remember, it's okay to add a little improv along the way.

Marriage isn't just a one-hit wonder - it's a chart-topping album with endless remixes. So, grab your partner, tune your instruments, and get ready for the encore of a lifetime. And hey, if you hit a few off-notes along the way, just remember, it's all part of the symphony!

SEVENTEEN

THE TODDLER TANGO

Imagine walking through a park, minding your own business, and suddenly, a random stranger runs up to you, gives you a bear hug, and starts ruffling your hair. Startling, right? Now, picture this from a child's perspective. Just because they're little doesn't mean they're okay with being grabbed, patted, or pinched on the cheek without a heads-up. Think of it this way: kids are tiny humans with personal boundaries. Asking them before you touch them isn't just polite - it's a golden ticket to teaching them about consent and respect.

By saying, "Hey, can I give you a high-five?" you're doing more than just checking in. You're showing them that their feelings matter, and they get to choose who gets up close and personal. And who knows? Maybe that polite request will save you from the wrath of sticky fingers or a surprise karate kick from a kid who's just not feeling it today.

Picture this: You've just landed on an alien planet. The inhabitants don't speak your language, and you don't speak theirs. How would you feel if they poked and prodded you like a specimen from Area 51? Not cool, right? Babies and toddlers are like those aliens. They might not have the vocabulary to say, "Back off, buddy!" but they sure have ways to show displeasure - crying, squirming, and yes, that epic meltdown in aisle three of the grocery store.

Behaving like a jerk to a child just because they can't articulate their feelings is akin to swatting at a kitten because it meows. It's uncool, unkind, and frankly, it's a one-way ticket to being labelled the neighbourhood grump. Instead, try tuning into their body language. If they lean away or seem uncomfortable, take the hint. Respecting their unspoken signals is not just decent behaviour - it's essential for building a foundation of trust and understanding. Plus, it saves you from getting an unexpected sticky lollipop stuck in your hair as an act of toddler rebellion.

Remember, a little asking goes a long way. It's not just about avoiding sticky situations (literally and figuratively), but about teaching the next generation the importance of consent and respect. And who knows? You might just become the favourite adult in the room - the one who gets the most enthusiastic high-fives and the biggest smiles, all because you took a moment to ask, rather than assume.

EIGHTEEN
THUMBS-UP

"High-fives and hugs require a thumbs-up, not just a run-up!" Life's playbook isn't always written in black and white; sometimes it's scribbled in the colourful crayon of human interaction. Imagine this: you're about to deliver a high-five to someone, and instead of reciprocating, they just stand there, expecting a magical connection to occur. Well, sorry buddy, but it takes two to tango, and in this case, two to slap hands with gusto. That's where the metaphorical "thumbs-up" comes in - it's the green light, the signal that says, "Yes, let's do this!" without it, you're just a lone ranger in a world of missed connections.

Now, let's talk hugs. Ah, the universal language of affection, right? Well, not quite. Picture this scene: you're bursting with enthusiasm, arms wide open, ready to envelop someone in a warm embrace, only to be met with a stiff, awkward stance. Awkward turtle, anyone? It's like trying to dance the tango with a partner who's forgotten the steps. A hug isn't just a physical act; it's a symphony of shared emotion, a duet of arms wrapping around each other in perfect harmony. Without that mutual agreement, you're left with a one-sided embrace that's about as comforting as a soggy sandwich.

So, why the insistence on a "thumbs-up"? Well, my friend, it's the secret sauce, the missing ingredient that turns a potential fumble into a touchdown. It's the non-verbal cue that says, "I see you, I acknowledge you, and I'm ready to engage." Without it, you're just flailing in the wind, hoping for a miracle. And let's face it, life's too short for awkward encounters and missed connections.

But fear not, dear reader, for there's hope yet! Next time you're gearing up for a high-five or gearing in for a hug, remember the golden rule: always wait for the thumbs-up. It's the difference between a memorable moment and a cringe-worthy catastrophe. So, give that thumbs-up, seal the deal, and embrace the chaos of human interaction with open arms - quite literally!

NINETEEN

TIME IS VALUABLE COMMODITY

Time is precious, so always ask for consent before hijacking someone's schedule.

Ah, time, that slippery eel we try to catch but always seem to lose hold of! Like a well-aged cheese or a fine wine, it's precious and should be treated with the utmost respect. But hey, just because time is precious doesn't mean we can't have a little fun with it, right? So here's a golden rule for you: 'Time is precious, so always ask for consent before hijacking someone's schedule.'

Let's unpack this, shall we? Picture this - you're cruising through your day, minding your own business, when suddenly, bam! Someone swoops in and hijacks your precious time. It's like being ambushed by a rogue pirate ship in the vast ocean of your schedule. Now, don't get me wrong, pirates can be cool and all, but when it comes to your time, it's best to be the captain of your own ship.

Asking for consent before hijacking someone's schedule is just good manners, really. It's like knocking on the door before barging into someone's room. You wouldn't want to catch them in their pyjamas, would you? Well, maybe you would, but that's a story for another time. The point is, respect other people's time like you'd respect a fine piece of art - with admiration and maybe a little awe.

Now, let's sprinkle in some humour, shall we? Picture this - you're about to hijack someone's schedule when suddenly, out of nowhere, a giant consent form appears in front of you. It's like a pop-up ad on the internet - annoying at first, but kind of hilarious when you think about it. So instead of just steamrolling over someone's plans, why not slide into their DMs with a polite request? Who knows, they might even say yes!

In the grand scheme of things, time is the ultimate currency. So let's spend it wisely and always ask for consent before hijacking someone's schedule. After all, a little courtesy goes a long way in this crazy, chaotic world we live in. And who knows, maybe one day, when you least expect it, someone will return the favour and ask for your consent before stealing a precious moment of your time."

TWENTY

ARE THEY COOL WITH IT?

Before you use someone's stuff, make sure they're cool with it.

As the old saying goes, "Don't dive into someone else's pool without checking the water temperature first!" This nugget of wisdom isn't just about swimming - it's a universal truth that applies to borrowing anything from a friend's hoodie to their Netflix password.

Imagine this - you're eyeing your buddy's prized collection of vintage comic books. They're practically begging to be read, right? But hold your horses! Before you go all sticky-fingered and snatch one for a quick read, it's crucial to establish whether your pal is cool with it. Sure, they might be totally chill about lending out their prized possessions, but there's also the chance they guard those comics with the fervour of a dragon hoarding gold. Best not to risk getting singed!

Let's not forget the modern-day minefield of digital borrowing. You're about to binge-watch the latest season of your favourite show, but alas, your subscription has expired. Fear not! Your bestie has graciously offered up their login details. But wait - before you hit "Sign In," send them a quick message. You don't want to end up on their "Blocked Users" list for eternity just because you assumed they wouldn't mind you piggybacking on their streaming service.

And what about that trusty stapler sitting on your coworker's desk? You know, the one that perfectly aligns the edges of your documents with a satisfying 'click.' It's tempting to sneak it over to your cubicle when they're on a coffee break, but resist the urge! A quick "Hey, mind if I borrow your stapler?" could save you from being labelled as the office stapler thief. Plus, it's a chance to bond over the finer points of office supplies. Who knew staplers could spark such riveting conversations?

So, whether it's physical belongings, digital access, or office supplies, remember the golden rule - always ask before you assume. It's not just about being polite; it's about preserving friendships, avoiding awkward confrontations, and maybe even discovering a shared love for obscure superhero comics or ergonomic staplers. After all, life's too short for unnecessary drama, especially when there are adventures to be had - responsibly, of course!

> *"Before you borrow, just ask, and don't assume your neighbour's lawnmower doubles as a community tool shed!"*

Imagine strolling through your neighbourhood, admiring the well-manicured lawns, when suddenly, your grass grows an inch taller. You realize your lawnmower is on the fritz. But wait! Your neighbour's lawnmower gleams invitingly in the sunlight. Before you seize it and embark on a mowing spree, pause! Remember, that lawnmower might be as personal to them as their morning coffee ritual or favourite pair of socks. Maybe it's the only thing keeping their sanity intact amidst the chaos of lawn maintenance. So, before you give it a spin, give them a ring. Who knows, they might even offer to mow your lawn for you, sparing you from potential mower mishaps!

> "*Think twice before claiming your colleague's snacks as office snacks, unless you're prepared for a snack showdown in the break room!*"

Ah, the communal office snack stash, a mysterious ecosystem where forgotten granola bars and elusive bags of chips reside. You spot a tempting treat with no name on it and assume it's fair game. But hold your munchies! That bag of chips might be a lifeline for your colleague during those midday slumps when caffeine just won't cut it. Plus, if you dare to indulge without permission, be prepared for a snack showdown worthy of the office gossip grapevine. Picture it - you and your coworker, facing off in the break room, armed with snack bags and a hunger for justice. So, next time you eye that unclaimed snack, remember, it's not just a bag of chips - it's a potential snack-time saga waiting to unfold.

> "*Before you wear your roommate's hoodie, make sure you're ready to negotiate a hoodie-sharing*

treaty!"

The allure of a cozy hoodie on a chilly day is undeniable, especially when it's conveniently hanging in your roommate's closet. But before you cozy up in their comfort, consider the unspoken bonds that bind roommates together. That hoodie might be their security blanket, their shield against the world's woes. And if you dare to do it without permission, be prepared to negotiate a hoodie-sharing treaty that could rival the most intense diplomatic negotiations. Picture yourself sitting down with your roommate, hoodie in hand, ready to discuss terms and conditions like a seasoned diplomat. Who knew a simple piece of clothing could spark such negotiations? So, before you borrow, just ask, and maybe offer to wash their dishes as a token of goodwill. After all, diplomatic relations are built on compromise - and clean kitchens.

TWENTY-ONE
HISTORY & EVOLUTION

Consent, the cornerstone of human interaction, has been interpreted and practised in myriad ways throughout history, reflecting the cultural and societal norms of different eras and civilizations. In ancient civilizations such as Mesopotamia and Ancient Egypt, consent was often a matter of familial or societal arrangement, with little consideration for individual agency, especially concerning marriage and sexual relations. However, there were exceptions, such as in Athenian democracy, where the concept of democratic governance extended to personal autonomy in some respects.

As societies evolved, so did notions of consent, albeit at varying paces and with differing degrees of recognition. The Middle Ages, characterized by feudalism and patriarchal structures, saw consent predominantly framed within the confines of male authority, particularly concerning matters of marriage and property. Women's autonomy was often subjugated to familial and societal expectations, with little regard for their individual desires or choices.

The legal evolution of consent mirrors the shifting attitudes and values of society over time. Key milestones in this evolution include landmark legal cases, legislative reforms, and social movements that have challenged and reshaped traditional conceptions of consent. One such milestone is the English common law doctrine of "consent to the harm," which emerged in the 19th century and recognized that consent could mitigate liability in certain contexts, such as contact sports or surgical procedures.

Another pivotal moment in the legal history of consent is the recognition of marital rape as a criminal offence. Historically, the concept of spousal immunity shielded perpetrators of sexual violence within marriage from prosecution. However, feminist movements in the 20th century challenged this notion, advocating for the recognition of women's bodily autonomy and the criminalization of marital rape. This led to significant legal reforms in many jurisdictions, affirming that marriage does not equate to blanket consent and that individuals have the right to refuse sexual activity, even within the bounds of matrimony.

Presently, consent laws vary across jurisdictions, reflecting diverse cultural, social, and legal contexts. In many countries, consent is a fundamental principle enshrined in both criminal and civil law, governing a wide range of interactions, from medical treatment to sexual relations. However, the interpretation and application of consent can vary significantly, leading to complex legal debates and challenges.

In cases involving sexual assault and rape, consent is a central issue, with the burden often placed on the prosecution to prove that consent was absent or invalid.

Legal frameworks differ in their definitions of consent, with some jurisdictions adopting affirmative consent standards, which require explicit, voluntary, and ongoing agreement throughout a sexual encounter. Others adhere to more traditional notions of consent, focusing on the absence of coercion or incapacity.

Despite advancements in legal protections, challenges persist in ensuring meaningful consent, particularly in cases involving vulnerable populations, such as minors, individuals with disabilities, or those subjected to coercion or duress. Moreover, cultural attitudes and societal norms continue to influence perceptions of consent, underscoring the ongoing need for education, advocacy, and legal reform to uphold the principles of autonomy, dignity, and respect for all individuals.

TWENTY-TWO
SOCIETAL DYNAMICS

Throughout history, patriarchal structures have often marginalized women's voices and agency, relegating them to subordinate roles within society. In such contexts, men typically held positions of power and authority, while women were expected to conform to societal norms and expectations, often at the expense of their own desires and autonomy. This power imbalance significantly influenced perceptions of consent, with women's consent often being overlooked or disregarded in favour of male privilege and entitlement.

"*In many cultures and legal systems, women's consent was implicitly assumed or deemed irrelevant, particularly within the context of marriage and sexual relations. The concept of marital rape, for instance, was largely unrecognized or dismissed, reflecting the belief that women were obligated to fulfil their marital duties regardless of their own wishes or desires. This pervasive notion not only perpetuated gender-based violence but also reinforced the notion that women's bodies were the property of their husbands, devoid of agency or autonomy.*"

Legal frameworks, historically shaped by patriarchal norms and attitudes, often prioritized male interests and perspectives over women's rights and well-being. Laws governing marriage, divorce, and inheritance, for example, frequently favoured men, further perpetuating gender inequality and reinforcing women's subordinate status within society. Moreover, legal standards for establishing consent in cases of sexual assault and rape were often inadequate, placing the burden on women to prove lack of consent rather than holding perpetrators accountable for their actions.

In recent decades, significant progress has been made in recognizing and addressing these systemic injustices. Feminist movements have challenged traditional notions of consent and advocated for legal reforms that prioritize women's autonomy and bodily integrity. The criminalization of marital rape, for instance, represents a significant milestone in acknowledging women's right to refuse sexual activity within marriage and holding perpetrators accountable for sexual violence.

Contemporary legal frameworks increasingly emphasize the importance of affirmative consent, which requires explicit, voluntary, and ongoing agreement throughout a sexual encounter. This shift reflects a broader recognition of women's agency and the importance of respecting their boundaries and choices. Moreover, legal reforms aimed at addressing gender-based violence, such as protective orders and support services for survivors, signal a growing commitment to prioritizing women's safety and well-being within the legal system.

However, despite these advancements, challenges persist in ensuring meaningful consent and addressing the underlying societal attitudes and norms that perpetuate gender inequality and violence against women. Education, advocacy, and cultural change are essential in challenging patriarchal structures and promoting a more equitable and just society where all individuals, regardless of gender, have the right to autonomy, dignity, and respect.

TWENTY-THREE
FUNDAMENTALS

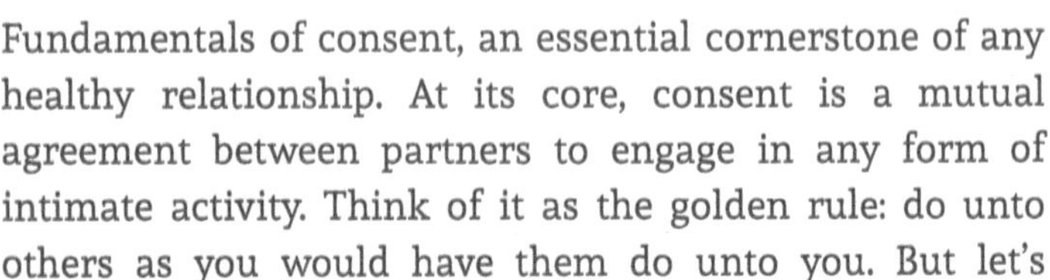

Fundamentals of consent, an essential cornerstone of any healthy relationship. At its core, consent is a mutual agreement between partners to engage in any form of intimate activity. Think of it as the golden rule: do unto others as you would have them do unto you. But let's unpack this concept further.

Firstly, clarity reigns supreme. Consent must be crystal clear, leaving no room for ambiguity or misinterpretation. This means both parties must be on the same page regarding what they're agreeing to. No blurred lines here - only a sharp, unequivocal "yes."

Voluntariness is the heartbeat of consent. It must be freely given, without coercion or pressure of any kind. Imagine a dance floor where both partners move in perfect synchrony, each step taken willingly and enthusiastically. That's the essence of voluntary consent.

Informed agreement adds another layer of depth. It's not just about saying "yes"; it's about understanding what you're saying yes to. Like signing a contract, consent requires full awareness of the terms and conditions. This includes being aware of any risks or consequences that may arise from the intimate activity.

Now, let's explore the different types of consent. There's explicit consent, where words explicitly express agreement - no room for guesswork here. Then there's implicit consent, where actions or behaviours imply agreement. Picture a knowing smile or a lingering touch that speaks volumes without uttering a single word.

Verbal consent involves vocalizing agreement - a straightforward "yes" or any other affirmative statement. Non-verbal consent, on the other hand, can be conveyed through gestures, body language, or even eye contact. It's all about tuning into your partner's cues and respecting their boundaries, whether they're spoken or unspoken.

Written consent takes things up a notch, putting pen to paper to document agreement. While it may seem formal, it can serve as a clear record of mutual consent, especially in more complex or high-risk situations. Oral consent, meanwhile, is spoken agreement, which, when communicated clearly, holds just as much weight.

Communication is the glue that holds the pillars of consent together. Effective communication strategies -such as active listening, empathy, and openness - lay the foundation for clear, mutual understanding. It's about creating a safe space where both partners feel comfortable expressing their desires, boundaries, and concerns.

Now, let's talk about the law. Breaking consent isn't just a breach of trust; it's a violation of basic human rights and, in many jurisdictions, a criminal offence. Laws vary by country, but in general, non-consensual sexual activity - whether through force, coercion, or incapacitation - is considered sexual assault or rape. Perpetrators can face severe legal consequences, including imprisonment and lifelong registration as a sex offender.

Consent isn't just a box to tick - it's the beating heart of intimacy, respect, and trust in any relationship. By understanding its fundamentals, communicating openly, and respecting each other's boundaries, partners can create a harmonious symphony of love and mutual pleasure, where every note is played with care and consent.

TWENTY-FOUR

SEXUAL RELATIONSHIPS

Consent in sexual relationships is a fundamental aspect of healthy, respectful interactions between partners. It's not merely about the absence of a 'no,' but rather the enthusiastic, ongoing agreement to engage in sexual activity. Understanding what constitutes consent is crucial. It involves clear communication and mutual understanding between all parties involved. Enthusiastic consent means that both partners are actively willing and excited to participate in the sexual encounter. It's about expressing desire and pleasure freely, without coercion or pressure.

Boundaries and negotiation play a significant role in the dynamics of sexual consent. Each individual has their own limits, preferences, and comfort levels when it comes to intimacy. Respectfully setting and respecting boundaries is essential for creating a safe and consensual sexual environment. This involves open and honest communication about desires, limits, and any concerns that may arise. Negotiating boundaries allows partners to find common ground and ensure that both parties feel comfortable and respected throughout the sexual encounter.

Addressing common misconceptions and myths surrounding sexual consent is vital for promoting a culture of understanding and respect. One prevalent misconception is the belief that silence or passivity implies consent. However, consent must be actively given, not assumed. Another myth is that consent is permanent and unchanging once given. In reality, consent can be withdrawn at any time, and it's essential to continuously check in with your partner to ensure their ongoing willingness and comfort.

Consent violations have serious emotional, psychological, and legal repercussions. When consent is disregarded or violated, it can lead to feelings of betrayal, trauma, and shame for the victim. Emotional and psychological consequences may include anxiety, depression, and post-traumatic stress disorder (PTSD). In addition to the personal impact, there are legal ramifications for individuals who break consent laws. In many jurisdictions, sexual assault and rape are punishable offences, carrying significant penalties including imprisonment and lifelong consequences such as being registered as a sex offender.

Understanding sexual consent goes beyond a simple 'yes' or 'no.' It requires ongoing communication, respect for boundaries, and enthusiastic agreement from all parties involved. Dispelling myths and misconceptions surrounding consent is crucial for promoting a culture of safety and respect. Consent violations have far-reaching consequences, both personally and legally, highlighting the importance of prioritizing consent in all sexual relationships.

TWENTY-FIVE
MEDICAL AND HEALTHCARE

Consent within medical and healthcare settings is a cornerstone principle that upholds patient autonomy, dignity, and rights. At its essence, consent involves the voluntary agreement by a patient to undergo medical treatment or procedures after being fully informed of the risks, benefits, and alternatives. This process, known as informed consent, ensures that patients are empowered to make decisions about their own bodies and healthcare.

"*Informed consent is not merely a formality but a legal and ethical requirement in medical practice. It serves to protect patients from unwanted interventions, potential harm, and violations of their bodily integrity. Without informed consent, medical procedures can potentially infringe upon a patient's rights and lead to legal consequences for healthcare providers.*"

Special cases within medical consent add layers of complexity to this principle. For minors, who may not have the legal capacity to provide consent, the involvement of parents or legal guardians becomes essential. However, depending on the circumstances and the minor's maturity level, they may be able to provide assent, indicating their willingness to participate in their healthcare decisions.

Similarly, mentally incapacitated individuals, such as those with severe cognitive impairments or mental illnesses, may face challenges in providing informed consent. In such cases, healthcare providers must follow established protocols, which may involve obtaining consent from legally authorized representatives or adhering to predetermined advance directives.

Ethical considerations play a crucial role in navigating the delicate balance between respecting patient autonomy and ensuring medical necessity. While patients have the right to refuse treatment, healthcare professionals must also consider the potential consequences of such decisions on the patient's health and well-being. Ethical dilemmas may arise when patients make choices that conflict with medical recommendations, prompting healthcare providers to engage in thoughtful discussions and, in some cases, seek legal guidance.

The legal framework surrounding consent varies across jurisdictions but generally requires healthcare providers to adhere to strict standards. Failure to obtain informed consent or proceeding with treatment against a patient's wishes can result in legal liabilities, including charges of medical malpractice or battery. In cases where consent is obtained under duress, coercion, or deception, it may be deemed invalid, further underscoring the importance of transparent communication and respect for patient autonomy.

Consent in medical and healthcare settings encompasses a complex interplay of legal, ethical, and moral considerations. By upholding the principles of informed consent, healthcare providers demonstrate respect for patient autonomy, foster trust in the patient-provider relationship, and mitigate the risk of potential harm or legal ramifications.

TWENTY-SIX

DIGITAL CONSENT

The digital age, where the concept of consent has taken on a whole new meaning, weaving its way through the intricate web of online interactions, privacy policies, and emerging technologies. Let's dive into this cybernetic sea and unravel the complexities of digital consent.

First up, we have the realm of online privacy and consent. In this digital landscape, our personal data is the currency, and consent is the gatekeeper. Think of it as the fine print in a contract - by agreeing to those terms and conditions, you're essentially giving your consent for companies to collect, store, and sometimes even share your information. However, the issue arises when these privacy policies are buried beneath layers of legalese, making it difficult for users to truly understand what they're agreeing to. This raises questions about the validity of consent in the digital realm and the need for transparent and user-friendly policies that empower individuals to make informed decisions about their data.

Now, let's navigate the winding pathways of social media and consent. Platforms like Facebook, Instagram, and Twitter have become virtual town squares where we share our thoughts, photos, and experiences with the world. But behind every post, like, and share lies the crucial element of consent. When we upload a picture of ourselves or tag our friends in a post, we're essentially giving consent for that information to be seen and potentially shared by others. However, the lines can blur when it comes to consent in the digital age. What happens when someone tags us in a photo without our permission, or when our personal information is shared in a group chat without our knowledge? These are the modern-day conundrums that require careful consideration of digital boundaries and consent.

> "*From artificial intelligence to virtual reality, these cutting-edge innovations have the power to reshape our digital landscape in profound ways. But with great power comes great responsibility, particularly when it comes to consent. Take AI, for example. Machine learning algorithms rely on vast amounts of data to function, but how do we ensure that this data is collected and used ethically and with the explicit consent of the individuals involved? Similarly, in virtual environments, where the lines between reality and simulation blur, how do we navigate issues of consent in interactions between digital avatars?*"

In the legal realm, breaking consent can have serious consequences. Laws and regulations such as the General Data Protection Regulation (GDPR) in Europe and the

California Consumer Privacy Act (CCPA) in the United States aim to protect individuals' privacy rights and ensure that companies obtain valid consent before collecting and processing personal data. Violating these laws can result in hefty fines and reputational damage for businesses.

Digital consent is a multifaceted concept that lies at the intersection of technology, privacy, and ethics. As we continue to navigate this brave new world of cyberspace, it's essential that we prioritize transparency, accountability, and respect for individuals' autonomy and digital rights. After all, in the digital age, consent isn't just a checkbox—it's the cornerstone of trust and integrity in our online interactions."

TWENTY-SEVEN
MENTAL HEALTH

In the realm of mental health and well-being, digital consent can serve as a lifeline, offering protection and support to those vulnerable to the harmful consequences of privacy breaches. Consider the scenario of someone grappling with mental health challenges, seeking solace and support in online communities or counselling platforms. For these individuals, the sanctity of their privacy is paramount - a breach of confidentiality could have devastating repercussions, potentially exacerbating feelings of isolation, shame, and despair.

"*Digital consent becomes a beacon of hope in these circumstances, providing individuals with the assurance that their personal information will be safeguarded and their privacy respected. By empowering users to explicitly grant consent before sharing sensitive data, whether it be in therapy sessions conducted via telehealth platforms or in online support groups, we create a protective barrier against unauthorized access and misuse of personal information. This not only fosters a sense of trust and security within digital spaces but also encourages individuals to seek the help they need without fear of judgment or exposure.*"

Moreover, the ramifications of privacy breaches extend far beyond the realm of mental health, encompassing issues such as cyberbullying, revenge porn, and online harassment. In cases where intimate images or personal details are shared without consent, the psychological toll can be immense, leading to feelings of violation, trauma, and even suicidal ideation. Digital consent mechanisms serve as a preemptive defence against such violations, allowing individuals to assert control over their digital footprint and protect themselves from harm.

In the unfortunate event that a privacy breach does occur, digital consent can also facilitate recourse and accountability. By clearly delineating the terms of consent and establishing protocols for reporting violations, individuals are better equipped to assert their rights and seek redress through legal channels. This not only serves as a deterrent to would-be perpetrators but also sends a powerful message that privacy violations will not be tolerated in the digital sphere.

In essence, digital consent is not merely a technicality or checkbox - it is a fundamental human right, essential for preserving dignity, autonomy, and well-being in an increasingly interconnected world. By championing the principles of informed consent, transparency, and user control, we can create safer, more equitable digital environments where individuals are empowered to navigate the complexities of cyberspace with confidence and resilience. And in doing so, we can help prevent tragedies, protect the vulnerable, and uphold the principles of dignity and respect for all.

TWENTY-EIGHT
EVERYDAY LIFE

The cornerstone of human interaction: consent. It's not just a legal concept; it's the glue that holds our social fabric together, ensuring that our interactions are respectful, dignified, and mutually beneficial. Let's delve into the intricate tapestry of consent in everyday life, exploring its nuances in social interactions, non-sexual physical contact, and the dynamics of authority.

> *"In the realm of social interactions, consent operates as a silent agreement, an unspoken contract that governs our relationships with friends, colleagues, and acquaintances. It's about respecting boundaries, both verbal and non-verbal, and recognizing cues that indicate comfort or discomfort. Whether it's deciding where to go for lunch or engaging in deep conversations, consent lays the foundation for trust and mutual respect."*

Now, let's talk about non-sexual physical contact - those hugs, handshakes, and pats on the back that punctuate our daily encounters. Here, consent becomes even more critical, as it involves navigating personal space and physical boundaries. What may be a friendly hug to one person could be an invasion of space to another. Understanding and respecting these boundaries is essential to fostering a culture of consent and ensuring that everyone feels safe and comfortable in their own skin.

But what about the murky waters of authority and consent? In workplaces, schools, and other hierarchies, power dynamics come into play, adding layers of complexity to the concept of consent. It's here that the law steps in, recognizing that consent given under duress or coercion is not truly consent at all. In legal terms, this is often referred to as "lack of capacity to consent," and it's a serious violation of individual rights.

In the workplace, for example, a supervisor may wield authority over their subordinates, creating a power imbalance that can make it difficult for employees to freely give or withhold consent. This is why many companies have strict policies against harassment and require explicit consent for any interactions that could be perceived as crossing professional boundaries.

Similarly, in educational settings, teachers and professors are entrusted with the well-being of their students, making it imperative that they respect boundaries and obtain consent before engaging in any activities that could be construed as inappropriate or invasive.

In essence, consent isn't just a checkbox to be ticked - it's a fundamental aspect of human dignity and autonomy. It requires active listening, empathy, and a genuine respect for the agency of others. By embedding consent into the fabric of our everyday interactions, we create a safer, more inclusive society where everyone's voice is heard and respected. And when it comes to the law, remember:

consent isn't just a suggestion - it's a legal requirement that ensures justice and equality for all.

TWENTY-NINE

EMOTIONAL PRESSURE

First and foremost, it's crucial to approach the situation with empathy and understanding. Recognise that the person you're inviting has their own desires, preferences, and boundaries, which may not always align with yours. By acknowledging their autonomy and agency, you create a space where they feel comfortable expressing their true feelings, whether they're enthusiastic about the invitation or hesitant to participate.

When asking for consent to include someone in a plan, it's essential to be clear, direct, and respectful. Instead of assuming their response or downplaying the significance of their decision, give them the opportunity to voice their thoughts openly and honestly. This might involve asking questions like, "Would you be interested in joining us for dinner tomorrow night?" or "Do you feel like going hiking this weekend?"

Furthermore, it's crucial to create an environment where the person feels empowered to say no without fear of judgment or reprisal. Expressing genuine understanding and appreciation for their decision, whatever it may be, helps to mitigate any feelings of guilt or obligation they may experience. Remember, consent should always be freely given, without any form of coercion or manipulation.

Now, let's address the elephant in the room: emotional pressure. It's natural to feel disappointed or frustrated if someone declines your invitation, especially if you've put effort into planning an event or activity. However, it's essential to manage your own emotions responsibly and avoid guilting or pressuring the other person into changing their mind.

Instead of resorting to emotional manipulation tactics like guilt-tripping or pleading, focus on fostering open communication and understanding. Acknowledge their decision with grace and dignity, and if appropriate, express that you would love to include them in future plans if they ever feel inclined to join.

In summary, asking for consent isn't just about obtaining a yes or no - it's about creating a space for open dialogue, mutual respect, and genuine understanding. By approaching the situation with empathy, clarity, and respect for the other person's autonomy, you can navigate these conversations with grace and integrity, fostering healthy relationships built on trust and mutual consent.

THIRTY

PSYCHOLOGICAL AND EMOTIONAL DIMENSIONS

When delving into the psychological and emotional dimensions of consent, we enter a realm where understanding, empathy, and respect are paramount. Personal boundaries form the bedrock of consent, serving as the invisible lines that delineate what is acceptable and what isn't within any interaction. These boundaries are unique to each individual, influenced by upbringing, culture, personal values, and past experiences. Understanding and respecting these emotional boundaries is crucial in fostering an environment where consent can be freely given and respected.

Trauma and past experiences wield a significant influence on how individuals perceive and engage with consent. The impact of past trauma can manifest in myriad ways, from triggering memories that cloud judgment to instilling deep-seated fears and anxieties. Survivors of trauma may find it challenging to assert their boundaries or navigate intimate situations, as their past experiences can create emotional barriers to freely giving consent. Recognizing and acknowledging the impact of past experiences is essential in creating a safe and supportive space where individuals feel empowered to communicate their boundaries without fear of judgment or re-traumatization.

> "*Empowerment lies at the heart of building confidence in asserting boundaries and giving consent. By equipping individuals with the knowledge, skills, and support they need to assert their autonomy, we foster a culture of respect and mutual understanding. Building confidence involves dismantling societal norms that perpetuate harmful myths about consent, such as the notion that silence implies consent or that consent can be coerced or manipulated. Instead, individuals must be empowered to advocate for their boundaries assertively and without apology, knowing that their voice matters and their autonomy is sacrosanct.*"

In the legal realm, breaking consent is a serious offence that carries significant consequences. Laws pertaining to consent vary by jurisdiction but typically encompass both verbal and non-verbal forms of communication. Consent must be explicit, informed, and freely given, without any form of coercion, manipulation, or incapacitation. Any violation of consent, whether through physical force, deception, or exploitation, constitutes a breach of trust and can result in criminal charges ranging from sexual assault to rape.

Moreover, the legal framework surrounding consent extends beyond the realm of sexual interactions to encompass various aspects of human interaction, including medical treatment, personal care, and contractual agreements. Consent forms the cornerstone of ethical and legal principles governing autonomy and bodily integrity, ensuring that individuals have the right to make informed decisions about their bodies and their lives.

In conclusion, understanding the psychological and emotional dimensions of consent requires a nuanced appreciation of personal boundaries, trauma, and empowerment. By fostering a culture of respect, empathy, and empowerment, we can create spaces where consent is freely given, respected, and protected under the law.

THIRTY-ONE

CHALLENGES AND CONTROVERSIES

Consent - a topic as intricate and nuanced as a spider's web, with each thread representing different facets of human interaction. Let's embark on a journey through the labyrinth of challenges and controversies surrounding consent, navigating through murky waters of intoxication, implicit versus explicit consent, and the complexities of power-imbalanced relationships.

First up, intoxication and consent. Picture this - a crowded party, music thumping, drinks flowing like a river. In such settings, alcohol and drugs can act as a fog, clouding judgment and blurring the lines of consent. But where do we draw the line between someone who's had a few too many and someone who's unable to give meaningful consent? Here, the law steps in with a stern voice, declaring that consent obtained under the influence of substances may not be valid. In legal terms, if an individual is incapacitated - unable to understand the nature of the act or to communicate their consent - it's a red flag. It's a reminder that in the eyes of the law, blurred vision doesn't mean blurred boundaries.

Next, let's delve into the intricate dance of implicit versus explicit consent. Explicit consent - the clear, unmistakable 'yes' - is often hailed as the gold standard. But what about those instances where words aren't spoken but signals are exchanged, where consent is implied through actions or body language? Here, we enter a grey area, a realm where interpretations can vary wildly. While some argue that non-verbal cues can convey consent just as effectively, others caution against assumptions, advocating for explicit verbal affirmation. In the legal arena, this debate rages on, with courts grappling with the complexities of deciphering intent and context.

And then there's the thorny issue of power-imbalanced relationships, where consent isn't just about desire but about dynamics. Consider the scenario of an employer and an employee, a teacher and a student - situations where one party wields authority over the other. Here, the spectre of coercion looms large, casting a shadow over the notion of the freely given consent. The law, recognizing the inherent vulnerability in such relationships, often imposes stricter standards, demanding clear evidence of voluntary agreement. It's a reminder that consent isn't just a checkbox to be ticked off but a delicate balance of power and autonomy.

Navigating the labyrinth of consent requires careful consideration of context, communication, and the law. It's a terrain fraught with challenges and controversies, where lines blur and boundaries shift. But amidst the complexity, one thing remains clear: consent is not just a legal concept but a cornerstone of respect, dignity, and human rights.

THIRTY-TWO

EDUCATING AND ADVOCATING FOR CONSENT

Let's dive deep into the ocean of consent, where every wave carries the weight of understanding, respect, and legality. At the heart of it, all lies a simple yet profound concept: 'I do' doesn't mean 'I always will' - check in for the encore! Now, this isn't just a catchy phrase; it's a cornerstone of healthy relationships, especially when it comes to matters as intimate as sex. Consent isn't a one-time deal; it's an ongoing dialogue, a continuous affirmation of mutual desire and respect.

"*To truly champion consent, we must start early, laying the foundation for a culture that values and respects personal boundaries. Educational programs are key here, providing comprehensive consent education in schools and communities. These programs go beyond the basics, delving into nuanced*

> *topics like enthusiastic consent, bodily autonomy, and understanding the power dynamics at play in relationships. By arming individuals with knowledge from a young age, we empower them to navigate the complexities of consent with confidence and clarity."*

But education doesn't stop in the classroom - it extends to the home as well. Parental guidance plays a crucial role in shaping attitudes towards consent. Parents have a responsibility to initiate open, honest conversations about consent, modelling healthy communication and respect within the family unit. By demystifying the topic and fostering a culture of consent at home, parents can equip their children with the tools they need to navigate relationships safely and responsibly.

Beyond education and familial influence, advocacy and policy change are vital components in the fight for consent culture. Activists and organizations work tirelessly to promote consent as a fundamental human right, lobbying for legislative changes that protect individuals from sexual coercion and abuse. Laws surrounding consent vary from region to region, but the essence remains the same: consent must be freely given, enthusiastic, and ongoing. Any violation of consent is not only morally reprehensible but also legally punishable.

In the eyes of the law, breaking consent is a serious offence, with consequences ranging from civil penalties to criminal charges. Whether it's sexual assault, harassment, or any other form of non-consensual behaviour, perpetrators can and should be held accountable for their actions. Consent isn't a grey area - it's black and white. If someone doesn't explicitly consent to a sexual act, it's non-negotiable. Period.

Advocating for consent isn't just a moral imperative - it's a legal one. By prioritizing consent education, fostering open dialogue at home, and advocating for policy change, we can cultivate a culture where 'I do' truly means 'I always will,' and where every encore is met with enthusiastic applause."

Case Study - I

Positive Examples - Stories where consent was effectively communicated and respected.

Let's delve and explore the depth of consent within marriage, along with the legal implications and real-life examples.

"Remember, 'I do' doesn't mean 'I always will' - check-in for the encore!" This statement encapsulates the essence of ongoing consent within a marital relationship. While marriage signifies a commitment to love and supports one another, it does not negate the need for continuous communication and mutual agreement, particularly in intimate matters such as sex. Despite saying 'I do' at the altar, partners should regularly check in with each other to ensure that their desires, boundaries, and comfort levels are respected.

In many legal jurisdictions, including those governed by common law, marriage does not imply automatic consent to sexual activity. Consent within marriage is governed by the same principles of autonomy and respect as consent outside of marriage. Engaging in sexual activity without the explicit consent of one's spouse constitutes sexual assault or rape, which is a serious criminal offence punishable by law.

ᐅᐅᐅ

Real-life stories and case studies serve as poignant reminders of the importance of consent within marriage -

Case Study: The "Spousal Rape" Case

In 1993, the United States Supreme Court addressed the issue of spousal rape in the landmark case of Oregon v. Rideout. The defendant, David Rideout, was charged with raping his estranged wife. Despite their marital status, the court ruled that marriage does not equate to irrevocable consent for sexual activity. Rideout was convicted of spousal rape, highlighting the legal recognition of consent within marriage and the consequences of violating it.

Open Communication and Mutual Respect

In contrast to cases of spousal rape, there are numerous examples of couples who prioritize open communication and mutual respect within their marital relationship. For instance, Jane and Michael have been married for ten years. They regularly engage in candid conversations about their sexual desires, boundaries, and fantasies. Before initiating any sexual activity, they seek verbal or non-verbal cues of consent from each other, ensuring that both parties are comfortable and enthusiastic. This commitment to ongoing consent strengthens their bond and fosters a healthy and fulfilling sexual relationship.

By exploring these real-life examples and legal precedents, it becomes evident that consent within marriage is not only a moral imperative but also a legal requirement. Partners must actively communicate and reaffirm consent to ensure that their intimate interactions are consensual and mutually satisfying.

ᐳᐳᐳ

The notable Indian case study addresses the issue of marital rape and the significance of consent within marriage -

Independent Thought v. Union of India (2017)

In the case of Independent Thought v. Union of India, the Supreme Court of India delivered a landmark judgment addressing the issue of marital rape and the age of consent within marriage. The Independent Thought case exemplifies the Indian judiciary's commitment to upholding the rights of women and children and underscores the significance of consent within marital relationships. By recognizing the inherent dignity and autonomy of individuals, irrespective of marital status, the judgment represents a significant step towards gender justice and social reform in India.

The case was brought before the Supreme Court by the non-governmental organization Independent Thought, challenging the exception to marital rape under the Indian Penal Code (IPC). Section 375 of the IPC, which defines rape, contains an exception clause stating that sexual intercourse by a man with his wife, not below 15 years, is not rape. This exception essentially legalizes sexual intercourse between a husband and wife, even if the wife is below the age of 18, the legal age of consent in India.

Key Arguments

Violation of Fundamental Rights - The petitioners argued that the exception to marital rape violated the fundamental rights of married girls, particularly their right to equality and dignity guaranteed under Articles 14 and 21 of the Indian Constitution. They contended that marriage should not be used as a license to perpetrate sexual violence against underage girls.

Child Rights Perspective - The case also emphasized the importance of protecting the rights of children and preventing child marriage, which is still prevalent in many parts of India. Allowing sexual intercourse with underage girls within marriage perpetuates the cycle of child marriage and undermines efforts to combat this social evil.

Supreme Court Judgment

In October 2017, the Supreme Court of India delivered a historic judgment in favor of Independent Thought, striking down the exception to marital rape under Section 375 of the IPC. The Court held that sexual intercourse with a minor wife, even if she is above 15 years of age, amounts to rape and is a criminal offence under the IPC.

Key Rulings and Impact

Protection of Minor Wives - The judgment provided much-needed legal protection to minor wives by criminalizing sexual intercourse with them, irrespective of marital status. This decision aimed to safeguard the rights and dignity of underage girls who were vulnerable to sexual exploitation within marriage.

Recognition of Consent - By invalidating the exception to marital rape, the Supreme Court reaffirmed the importance of consent within marriage. The judgment emphasized that marriage does not imply perpetual consent to sexual activity and underscored the need for mutual respect and autonomy between spouses.

Addressing Child Marriage - The judgment also highlighted the link between child marriage and sexual violence, calling for concerted efforts to eradicate this harmful practice. By criminalizing sexual intercourse with minor wives, the Court aimed to deter child marriage and promote the welfare of young girls.

Case Study - 11

Negative Examples: Cases of consent violations and their consequences.

"Let's delve into the heart of this statement: 'Remember, 'I do' doesn't mean 'I always will' - check in for the encore!' This isn't just a catchy phrase; it's a profound reminder that marriage isn't a stagnant vow locked in time but rather a dynamic, evolving commitment that requires constant nurturing. At its core, this sentiment extends beyond the realms of love and partnership - it echoes the importance of ongoing consent, particularly in the realm of physical intimacy.

Consent, both within and outside of marriage, is a fundamental aspect of human relationships. It's the cornerstone of respect, trust, and mutual understanding. However, the misconception that marriage implies perpetual consent has led to dire consequences in many cases. People assume that once they say 'I do,' they've granted a blanket approval for all future sexual encounters. But here's the truth: consent isn't a one-time deal. It's a continuous dialogue, a reaffirmation of desire and boundaries, each and every time.

Now, let's talk law. In many jurisdictions, the legal landscape surrounding consent is crystal clear: without explicit, enthusiastic consent, any sexual activity constitutes assault or rape. Marriage doesn't exempt individuals from this principle. No means no, whether you're married or not. And just because someone said 'I do' at the altar doesn't mean they've forfeited their right to say

"

'no' in the bedroom.

Real-life stories and case studies drive this point home with painful clarity. Take, for instance, the case of Jane and John. They were the picture-perfect couple, married for years, until John began to view Jane's consent as a given. He assumed that because they were married, he had a perpetual green light for intimacy. But Jane's feelings and boundaries were disregarded, leading to years of emotional turmoil and, eventually, a legal battle for divorce on grounds of sexual assault.

Or consider the case of Michael and Sarah, high school sweethearts turned spouses. Sarah had always been vocal about her boundaries, but after marriage, Michael began to ignore her protests, citing their marital status as a justification for his actions. Sarah felt trapped, powerless to assert her autonomy within the confines of their relationship. It wasn't until she sought legal counsel that she realized her rights hadn't evaporated upon saying 'I do.'

These stories serve as cautionary tales, highlighting the dangers of assuming perpetual consent within marriage. Consent isn't a contractual obligation; it's a sacred trust that must be honored and respected, regardless of relationship status. And the law, thankfully, stands as a beacon of justice for those who've had their autonomy violated. Marriage may be a lifelong commitment, but it's not a blank check for sexual entitlement. So, remember, the encore isn't just a performance - it's a reaffirmation of consent, each and every time."

ゆゆゆ

A notable Indian case study that addresses the

issue of marital rape and the significance of consent within marriage -

One of the most infamous cases in India that highlighted the importance of consent within marriage is the case of "State of Maharashtra v. Madhkar Narayan Mardikar" in 1991. This landmark case brought to light the issue of marital rape and challenged the prevailing notion that marriage implied irrevocable consent to sexual intercourse.

In this case, Madhkar Narayan Mardikar was charged with raping his wife, Rekha, multiple times over the course of their marriage. Rekha, after enduring years of abuse, finally gathered the courage to file a complaint against her husband. The prosecution argued that marital rape should be recognized as a criminal offence, regardless of the marital status of the individuals involved. They contended that consent must be freely given by both parties, even within the confines of marriage.

The defence, on the other hand, relied on the prevailing legal doctrine that exempted husbands from being charged with rape within marriage. They argued that by marrying her husband, Rekha had consented to sexual intercourse for the duration of their marriage, and therefore, the charges against Mardikar should be dismissed.

The case sparked widespread debate and controversy, igniting discussions about women's rights, marital obligations, and the legal definition of rape in India. Ultimately, the Supreme Court of India delivered a historic judgment, ruling in favor of Rekha and affirming that marriage did not equate to automatic consent for sexual activity.

The court's decision was a watershed moment in India's legal landscape, setting a precedent for future cases involving marital rape and reinforcing the principle that consent is paramount, regardless of marital status. The case also prompted lawmakers to reconsider existing laws and advocate for legislative reforms to better protect victims of domestic violence and sexual assault within marriage.

The State of Maharashtra v. Madhkar Narayan Mardikar case serves as a stark reminder of the importance of recognizing and respecting individual autonomy and bodily integrity within the institution of marriage. It stands as a testament to the power of the law to uphold justice and safeguard the rights of vulnerable individuals, even in the face of entrenched societal norms and prejudices.

ᐅᐅᐅ

Lesson Learned

The case of "State of Maharashtra v. Madhkar Narayan Mardikar" and other similar stories teach us several crucial lessons about improving consent practices, particularly within the context of marriage. By learning from these stories and implementing these practices, society can move towards a more just and respectful understanding of consent within marriage. This shift not only protects individuals but also strengthens the foundation of marital relationships, making them more equitable and loving.

Continuous and Explicit Consent

"Consent is an ongoing process and must be explicitly obtained every time. Couples should

regularly communicate their boundaries and preferences, ensuring that both partners feel comfortable and respected."

Legal Recognition of Marital Rape

"Legal systems must recognize that marriage does not nullify an individual's right to refuse sex. Advocacy for legal reforms to criminalize marital rape and ensure that laws protect all individuals, regardless of their marital status, is crucial."

Educational Initiatives

"Many people are unaware of the nuances of consent, especially within marriage. Implementing comprehensive sex education programs that cover consent, respectful relationships, and legal rights from a young age is essential."

Empowerment and Support for Victims

"Victims of marital rape often feel powerless and isolated. Strengthening support systems, including legal aid, counseling services, and support groups, can empower victims to speak out and seek justice."

Cultural Change

"Societal norms and cultural attitudes often perpetuate the myth of perpetual consent within marriage. Promoting cultural change through public awareness campaigns that challenge harmful

stereotypes and emphasize the importance of mutual respect and consent in all relationships is necessary."

Judicial Sensitivity and Training

"Judges and law enforcement officers need to be sensitive to the realities of marital rape. Providing specialized training for the judiciary and law enforcement on handling cases of marital rape with the sensitivity and seriousness they deserve is important."

Encouraging Open Communication

"Many issues of consent arise from a lack of open and honest communication between partners. Encouraging couples to engage in regular, open dialogues about their needs, desires, and boundaries fosters a relationship based on mutual understanding and respect."

Policy Implementation and Monitoring

"Simply having laws in place is not enough; they must be effectively implemented and monitored. Ensuring robust mechanisms for the implementation and monitoring of laws related to consent and sexual assault, with accountability measures for enforcement agencies, is crucial."

Role of Healthcare Providers

"*Healthcare providers often encounter victims of marital rape and can play a crucial role in support and intervention. Training healthcare providers to recognize signs of marital rape and provide appropriate support and referrals to legal and counselling services is essential.*"

Case Study - III

Case Study on Consent - Reel Life and Real Life

Consent is a fundamental concept in sexual ethics, asserting that all parties involved in any sexual activity must willingly agree to participate. This case study examines the portrayal of consent in the movies and contrasts it with real-life incidents to highlight the importance and complexities of the "No Means No" principle.

"Reel Life - "The Accused" (1988)"

"The Accused," directed by Jonathan Kaplan and starring Jodie Foster and Kelly McGillis, is a courtroom drama based on the real-life gang rape of Cheryl Araujo in New Bedford, Massachusetts, in 1983. Jodie Foster plays Sarah Tobias, a young woman who is gang-raped by several men in a bar while onlookers cheer them on. The film follows the legal battle to bring the perpetrators to justice. The film delves into societal tendencies to blame victims of sexual assault based on their behaviour, appearance, or past. Sarah faces judgment and prejudice from those who believe she "asked for it" due to her appearance and behaviour. The narrative portrays the difficulties in prosecuting rape cases, especially when the victim's character is put on trial. Despite the challenges, the film emphasizes the importance of fighting for justice and the empowerment that comes from standing up against one's attackers. "The Accused" received critical acclaim for its unflinching portrayal of rape and its aftermath, sparking discussions about the treatment of rape victims in the judicial system and society.

"Real Life Incident - The Nirbhaya Case"

On December 16, 2012, a young woman, later referred to as Nirbhaya, was brutally gang-raped and assaulted on a bus in Delhi. She succumbed to her injuries thirteen days later. This heinous crime shocked the nation and led to massive protests and demands for stricter laws on sexual violence. The incident led to significant amendments in Indian laws regarding sexual assault. The Criminal Law (Amendment) Act, 2013, introduced stricter penalties for sexual crimes and expanded the definition of rape. The case brought the issue of sexual violence into the public discourse, highlighting the need for societal change in attitudes towards women and consent. The perpetrators were convicted and sentenced to death, a verdict that was upheld by the Supreme Court. This case reinforced the message that sexual violence would not be tolerated and that victims would receive justice.

"Additional Real-Life Examples"

In the Steubenville High School rape case (2012), two high school football players were convicted of raping a 16-year-old girl, with the assault recorded and shared on social media. The case brought national attention to the role of digital consent and highlighted the need for educating young people about consent. In the Stanford University rape case (2015), Brock Turner assaulted an unconscious woman, receiving a controversial six-month jail sentence. The light sentence prompted public outcry and led to legislative changes in California to ensure harsher penalties for similar crimes. The Harvey Weinstein scandal (2017) saw dozens of women accuse the Hollywood producer of sexual harassment, assault, and rape, leading to his conviction and the rise of the #MeToo movement. This case underscored the systemic abuse of power in the entertainment industry and the importance of holding perpetrators accountable.

"*Reel Life - "Pink" Movie*"

"Pink," directed by Aniruddha Roy Chowdhury and released in 2016, is a Bollywood film that addresses the issue of sexual consent and the societal stigma faced by women who assert their rights. The film stars Amitabh Bachchan as a lawyer defending three young women—Minal (Taapsee Pannu), Falak (Kirti Kulhari), and Andrea (Andrea Tariang)—who are accused of attempted murder after one of them, Minal, hits a man named Rajveer in self-defence. The movie's central theme revolves around the concept of consent, emphasizing that "no means no," regardless of the circumstances. It showcases the biases present in the judicial system and society at large, where the victim's character is often questioned rather than the perpetrator's actions. Through the legal battle, the movie emphasizes the importance of standing up for one's rights and fighting against patriarchal norms. "Pink" was lauded for its bold take on a sensitive issue and sparked widespread discussions about consent in India. The film's powerful dialogue, especially the monologue delivered by Bachchan's character, became a cultural touchstone.

"*The portrayal of consent in "Pink" and "The Accused," alongside real-life cases such as the Nirbhaya case, the Steubenville High School rape case, the Stanford University rape case, and the Harvey Weinstein scandal, underscores the critical importance of understanding and respecting consent. These narratives and incidents highlight pervasive issues of victim blaming, societal bias, and the need for robust legal protections for survivors of sexual violence. The principle that "no means no" is essential for ensuring justice and fostering a culture of respect and equality. Through media representation and real-life legal reforms, progress can be made in ensuring justice for victims and preventing sexual violence. This case study underscores the need for continuous education and dialogue about consent, empowerment, and the eradication of gender-based violence, aiming for a society where "no" unequivocally means "no."*"

Conclusion

Advocate for Consent and Fostering a Culture of Respect

As we conclude this exploration of consent in every aspect of life and society, it's imperative that we reflect on the lessons we've learned and consider how we can actively apply them in our daily lives. Understanding consent is not just an intellectual exercise; it's a call to action. Each of us has a role to play in advocating for consent and contributing to a culture of respect and mutual understanding.

First and foremost, we must embrace the concept of continuous and explicit consent. This means recognizing that consent is an ongoing dialogue, not a one-time event. Whether in intimate relationships, friendships, workplaces, or public interactions, we must ensure that we are always respectful of others' boundaries and preferences. By regularly checking in with those around us and fostering open communication, we can create environments where everyone feels safe and valued.

Advocating for legal reforms is another crucial step. As we've seen, the legal system often lags behind societal needs, and it is up to us to push for changes that protect the rights and dignity of all individuals. This includes advocating for the recognition and criminalization of marital rape, ensuring that victims of sexual assault have access to justice, and demanding that consent laws are clear and enforced. By supporting legislative efforts and holding our representatives accountable, we can make meaningful strides toward a more just society.

> *"Education is a powerful tool in promoting a culture of consent. Comprehensive sex education that includes lessons on consent, respect, and healthy relationships should be a staple in our educational systems. As parents, educators, and community leaders, we have the responsibility to ensure that young people understand the importance of consent and are equipped with the knowledge to practice it in their lives. By fostering early awareness, we lay the groundwork for future generations to build relationships based on mutual respect and understanding."*

Support systems for victims of consent violations are essential. Empowering victims to speak out and seek justice requires robust support networks, including legal aid, counseling, and advocacy groups. By volunteering, donating, or simply being a supportive friend, we can help create a community where victims feel heard and validated. This collective support is vital in breaking the silence and stigma that often surrounds issues of consent and assault.

Cultural change starts with each of us. Challenging harmful stereotypes, speaking out against inappropriate behavior, and promoting respectful interactions are actions we can all take. Public awareness campaigns and community initiatives can amplify these efforts, shifting societal norms towards a culture that prioritizes consent and respect. Each time we advocate for these values, we contribute to a broader movement that seeks to reshape our cultural landscape.

Moreover, training and sensitizing those in positions of authority, such as judges, law enforcement officers, and healthcare providers, is critical. These professionals play a pivotal role in the lives of those affected by consent violations, and their understanding and sensitivity can make a significant difference. By supporting specialized training programs and advocating for systemic changes, we can ensure that victims receive the care and justice they deserve.

"Encouraging open communication is fundamental. In all our relationships, we should strive to maintain honest and respectful dialogues about our needs, desires, and boundaries. This practice not only strengthens our connections but also reinforces the importance of mutual consent in every interaction. By modeling this behavior, we set a positive example for others and contribute to a culture where consent is the norm."

Finally, implementation and monitoring of consent-related policies are crucial. Having laws in place is not enough; we must ensure they are effectively enforced and that there are mechanisms for accountability. By staying informed, participating in civic duties, and supporting organizations that monitor these issues, we can help maintain the integrity of consent laws and practices.

In conclusion, promoting a culture of respect and consent requires a multifaceted approach that involves education, advocacy, support, and personal responsibility. By applying what we've learned, advocating for change, and fostering open communication, we can build a society where every individual's autonomy and dignity are upheld. Let us commit to being champions of consent, creating a world where respect and mutual understanding are at the forefront of all our interactions.

Suggestions For More Information About Conset

Some Movies on Consent

"The Accused" (1988, USA)
- Director: Jonathan Kaplan
- Synopsis: A powerful film starring Jodie Foster, which delves into the legal and emotional aftermath of a sexual assault case, highlighting the importance of consent and the challenges victims face in seeking justice.
- Critical Acclaim: Foster won the Academy Award for Best Actress for her role.

"Elle" (2016, France)
- Director: Paul Verhoeven
- Synopsis: A provocative thriller featuring Isabelle Huppert as a woman who, after being raped in her home, takes an unconventional approach to dealing with the aftermath. The film explores complex themes of consent, power, and control.
- Critical Acclaim: Nominated for the Academy Award for Best Foreign Language Film, and Huppert won the Golden Globe for Best Actress.

"Margarita with a Straw" (2014, India)
- Director: Shonali Bose
- Synopsis: The story of a young woman with cerebral palsy who explores her sexuality and seeks an understanding of consent and personal autonomy in her relationships.
- Critical Acclaim: Won the NETPAC Award for World or International Asian Film Premiere at the Toronto International Film Festival.

"Thelma" (2017, Norway)

- Director: Joachim Trier

- Synopsis: A supernatural thriller about a young woman who discovers her suppressed desires and supernatural abilities, exploring themes of consent, repression, and self-discovery.

- Critical Acclaim: Norway's submission for the Best Foreign Language Film at the Academy Awards, critically acclaimed for its direction and storytelling.

"A Fantastic Woman" (2017, Chile)

- Director: Sebastián Lelio

- Synopsis: Follows Marina, a transgender woman, as she faces societal prejudice and fights for her right to mourn her lover. The film touches on themes of consent, identity, and respect.

- Critical Acclaim: Won the Academy Award for Best Foreign Language Film.

"Promising Young Woman" (2020, USA)

- Director: Emerald Fennell

- Synopsis: A dark comedy thriller about a woman who seeks to avenge her best friend, who was a victim of rape. The film explores themes of consent, revenge, and the consequences of a society that often dismisses sexual assault.

- Critical Acclaim: Won the Academy Award for Best Original Screenplay and was nominated for several other Oscars, including Best Picture and Best Director.

"The Nightingale" (2018, Australia)

- Director: Jennifer Kent

- Synopsis: Set in 1825, this brutal historical drama follows a young Irish convict woman seeking revenge for the brutalization of her family. It tackles themes of consent, colonialism, and systemic violence.

- Critical Acclaim: Won the Special Jury Prize at the Venice Film Festival, noted for its powerful performances and unflinching portrayal of violence and its impact.

"The Invisible Man" (2020, USA/Australia)

- Director: Leigh Whannell
- Synopsis: A modern reimagining of the classic tale, focusing on a woman who believes she is being stalked by her abusive and supposedly deceased ex-boyfriend. The film addresses consent, control, and gaslighting.
- Critical Acclaim: Praised for its tense atmosphere and Elisabeth Moss's compelling performance, it received strong critical and audience acclaim.

"Anatomy of a Scandal" (2021, UK)

- Director: David E. Kelley, Melissa James Gibson
- Synopsis: A British drama series that follows a high-profile parliamentary minister whose life unravels when he is accused of rape. The series examines the nuances of consent, power, and public perception.
- Critical Acclaim: Received positive reviews for its thought-provoking storyline and strong performances.

"Spring Breakers" (2012, USA)

- Director: Harmony Korine
- Synopsis: A crime drama that follows four college girls who rob a restaurant to fund their spring break trip. The film explores themes of consent, exploitation, and the hedonistic pursuit of pleasure.
- Critical Acclaim: Noted for its provocative style and performances, especially James Franco's role, it sparked discussions about youth culture and consent.

ᛈᛈᛈ

Some Books on Consent

"Asking for It: The Alarming Rise of Rape Culture - and What We Can Do about It"by Kate Harding
- Synopsis: Harding provides a thorough examination of rape culture and its pervasive effects, offering insight into how society can change to better understand and respect consent.
- Critical Acclaim: Praised for its clear, compelling, and often personal exploration of a critical issue.

"Know My Name"by Chanel Miller
- Synopsis: A memoir by the woman previously known as Emily Doe in the Brock Turner sexual assault case. Miller's powerful narrative sheds light on her experience and the broader implications for consent and justice.
- Critical Acclaim: Highly acclaimed for its raw honesty and impactful storytelling, winning the National Book Critics Circle Award for Autobiography.

"The Consent Guidebook: A Practical Approach to Consensual, Respectful, and Enthusiastic Interactions" by Erin Tillman
- Synopsis: A practical guide to understanding and practicing consent in everyday interactions, offering tools and advice for fostering a consent culture.
- Critical Acclaim: Praised for its accessible and practical approach to a crucial topic.

"Blurred Lines: Rethinking Sex, Power, and Consent on Campus" by Vanessa Grigoriadis
- Synopsis: An investigative look at the complexities of consent on college campuses, examining how students navigate sex, power, and consent in contemporary society.

- Critical Acclaim: Noted for its thorough research and balanced perspective on a controversial issue.

"Missoula: Rape and the Justice System in a College Town" by Jon Krakauer

- Synopsis: An investigative work that examines several cases of sexual assault at the University of Montana, exploring the systemic issues in handling rape and consent.
- Critical Acclaim: Krakauer's work is critically acclaimed for its meticulous research and gripping narrative, sparking national conversations about consent and justice.

"Consent: A Memoir of Unwanted Attention" by Donna Freitas

- Synopsis: A deeply personal memoir in which Donna Freitas recounts her experience with unwanted attention from a professor during her graduate studies. The book explores the complexities of power dynamics, academic life, and the lasting impact of non-consensual behaviour.
- Critical Acclaim: Praised for its candid and thoughtful examination of harassment and the long-term effects of violations of consent.

"The Right to Sex: Feminism in the Twenty-First Century" by Amia Srinivasan

- Synopsis: A collection of essays that delve into contemporary issues surrounding sex, power, and consent. Srinivasan explores the political and personal dimensions of sexual desire, consent, and feminist theory.
- Critical Acclaim: Celebrated for its intellectual rigour and engaging prose, offering nuanced perspectives on complex topics.

"Rage Becomes Her: The Power of Women's Anger" by Soraya Chemaly

- Synopsis: This book examines the ways in which women's anger is often suppressed and stigmatized, and how acknowledging and channelling this anger can be a powerful force for change. It discusses consent in the context of emotional and physical boundaries.

- Critical Acclaim: Acclaimed for its insightful and empowering message, encouraging women to reclaim their anger and assert their boundaries.

"Consent on Campus: A Manifesto" by Donna Freitas

- Synopsis: Freitas offers a comprehensive look at the culture of consent on college campuses, analyzing the challenges and proposing solutions for creating a safer, more respectful environment. The book combines research, personal stories, and practical advice.

- Critical Acclaim: Recognized for its thorough research and practical approach to improving consent education and policies on campuses.

"Girls & Sex: Navigating the Complicated New Landscape" by Peggy Orenstein

- Synopsis: Orenstein explores the sexual lives of teenage girls, examining how they navigate issues of consent, pleasure, and agency in a culture often dominated by contradictory messages. The book draws on extensive interviews and research.

- Critical Acclaim: Widely praised for its candid and compassionate exploration of young women's experiences, offering important insights for parents, educators, and policymakers.

ppp

References Of Case Study

1. Consent within Marriage
- Legal implications and real-life examples
- Source: No specific reference provided, but it encompasses legal principles and examples from various jurisdictions.
2. Case Study: Oregon v. Rideout (1993)
- Spousal rape case illustrating non-consent within marriage.
- Source: Oregon v. Rideout (1993) Supreme Court case.
3. Positive Example of Consent in Marriage:
- Example of Jane and Michael's healthy marital communication and respect for consent.
- Source: No specific reference provided, likely hypothetical.
4. Indian Case Study: Independent Thought v. Union of India (2017):
- Landmark Indian Supreme Court case addressing marital rape and consent.
- Source: Independent Thought v. Union of India (2017) Supreme Court case.
5. Negative Examples of Consent Violations:
- Illustration of cases where consent was violated within marriage.
- Source: Hypothetical examples provided.
6. Indian Case Study: State of Maharashtra v. Madhkar Narayan Mardikar (1991):
- Landmark Indian case addressing marital rape and consent.
- Source: State of Maharashtra v. Madhkar Narayan Mardikar (1991) Supreme Court case.
7. Lessons Learned from the Case:
- Recommendations for improving consent practices within

marriage.
- Source: No specific reference provided, likely based on legal and sociocultural analyses.

8. The Nirbhaya Case
- BBC News. (2013). [India gang rape: Six men charged with murder]
- The Guardian. (2017). [How a gang rape and murder shook Delhi – and the world]

9. The Steubenville High School Rape Case
- CNN. (2013). [Steubenville: Aftermath of the verdict]
- The New York Times. (2013). [Steubenville Teenagers Guilty in Rape That Social Media Brought to Light]

10. The Stanford University Rape Case
- NPR. (2016). [Stanford Rape Case: Read The Full Text Of The Judge's Sentencing Decision]
- BuzzFeed News. (2016). [Here's The Powerful Letter The Stanford Victim Read To Her Attacker]

11. The Harvey Weinstein Scandal
- The New York Times. (2017). [Harvey Weinstein Paid Off Sexual Harassment Accusers for Decades]
- BBC News. (2020). [Harvey Weinstein found guilty of rape]

Ashish Shekhar
FilmFreeway/AshishShekhar
Instagram: *calmly_calloff*
& flickmotionspictures
ashishshekhar82@gmail.com
+91 9699523251